ENVIRONMENT AT THE CROSSROADS

T0294442

Also available from Carcanet Press and the
Fundação Calouste Gulbenkian

The State of the World
The Urgency of Theory
Is Science Nearing Its Limits?
Can There Be Life Without the Other?

Environment at the Crossroads

CARCANET

and

FUNDAÇÃO
CALOUSTE
GULBENKIAN

First published in Great Britain in 2010 by
Carcanet Press Limited
Alliance House
Cross Street
Manchester M2 7AQ

Co-published with Fundação Calouste Gulbenkian

FUNDAÇÃO
CALOUSTE
GULBENKIAN

A CIP catalogue record for this book is available from the British Library
ISBN 978 1 84777 119 3

Set in Monotype Dante by XL Publishing Services, Tiverton
Printed and bound in England by SRP Ltd, Exeter

Contents

Foreword

Foundations can and should be the agents of the future. During the conferences that I usually promote in the last week of October, I have tried to create a moment of reflection and clear debate on the great issues of our time. In this regard, the global environmental crisis is a prime example of a crossroad between the past and the future and a source of immediate demands in the decisions of the present.

The importance of this conference and the opportunity it presents are self-evident, as in less than a month's time the 15th Conference of the Parties for the United Nations Framework Convention for Climate Change will take place. Next December, in Copenhagen, the States are going to define a new international regime for climate change in the long term, after 2012, looking ahead to 2020 and even 2050.

Faced with the difficulties ahead and the tendency to make minimal commitments, as we were alerted by Bill McKibben last September (Review, *Guardian*, 26 September 2009), we see that more than an agreement, the world needs a solution.

Our Conference, however, doesn't deal exclusively with the

climate change theme, but rather places it where it makes sense, that is, within a wider framework that has been recognised for longer, the global environmental crisis. In this sense, we will listen to and debate different approaches to this crisis and crossroad, as when dealing with the environment, we deal also with an overall crisis and crossroad of culture and civilisation. It is a crisis that also challenges our values and our certainties regarding our institutions and even our daily habits; such is the case in the consumption sphere. In fact, environmental issues have an eminently public and collective nature, but are also related to behaviours, the day-to-day lives of citizens and their sphere of individual responsibility.

Our relationship with nature has an intrinsic ethical component, the relationship between the selfishness of our comfort and our human solidarity. If we don't re-encounter the fundamental necessary balance, we might go rapidly from the city to the desert, from harmony to catastrophe.

Over the next couple of days we will debate in the four main conferences, as well as the three thematic panels, the different facets of the global environmental crisis, as well as the complex relationships among these different dimensions: the acceleration of the process of reduction in the diversity of habitats and flora and fauna species; the agricultural dilemma between the need for food and energy production and the conservation of the countryside and the ecosystems; the growing scarcity and degradation that attack both fresh water – with the increased pressure of consumption for farming and livestock production and the growing needs of the emerging countries – and the great ocean ecosystems, where loss of biological productivity runs in parallel with the increase in temperature and growing acidity of the seas.

We will also discuss the complex problems, not just of the reconstruction of the productive systems but, mainly, of the necessary changes in the paradigm of economic and financial thinking, if we don't want to transform the return to growth to the mere return to old habits and practices that ignore environmental limits, the unequal distribution of wealth and the imperative of effective sustainability.

Another indispensable subject, which is at the centre of this

Conference's concerns, consists of the search for better public policies; this will not only allow for a response to the plural diagnosis of the environmental crisis, but will further advance the strategy to combat and overcome it. How to modify models, mechanisms and governance processes at local, regional and national levels? How to increase the international cooperation that, while guaranteeing the transition to sustainable development, also allows for an increase in the possibilities of long-lasting peace, without which no future worthy of this name will be possible?

The most visible and imperative part of the environmental crisis, the challenge of climate change, is one of our concerns in this conference. What is at stake is decisive, as we can no longer completely avoid climate change. The prevention phase was, unfortunately, wasted and has passed. Everything indicates that an average increase of 2°C is a given fact, even if, by a miracle, the greenhouse gases emissions were to cease right now. But there's a difference between a change of more than 2°C and more than 4°C. The difference between a change we can adapt to and that which may eventually destroy us.

This Conference does not constitute an isolated action but rather is a part of the Foundation's priority interventions being developed in different initiatives. The Gulbenkian Environment Programme, launched in 2007, aims to contribute to fundamental public awareness regarding environmental issues and their respective effects in the most varied aspects of human life. Its role is in increasing research; promoting the transfer of knowledge to technologies with less environmental impact and more efficient use of energy and resources; facilitating the demonstration of good practices from an environmental perspective, in terms of better management of processes and organisations; and, finally, strengthening the cooperation and dialogue between the different players – public, private and civil society in the formulation of public policies. There is also the International Calouste Gulbenkian Prize, which every two years aims to award innovative actions in terms of respect for biodiversity, defence of the environment and humankind's relationship with nature. I could also highlight other projects, such as those developed where the environment intersects with health, the partnerships with the European Environment Agency and the European Commission's Joint Research Centre and, from next year, with the Energy and Resources Institute in India, directed by Rajendra Pachauri, who chairs the United Nations Intergovernmental Panel for Climate Change.

A very practical example of the Foundation's concern regarding environmental issues is that, thanks to the changes we introduced, this building was considered energetically efficient under the scope of the European Commission's Greenbuilding Programme.

The Calouste Gulbenkian Foundation's environmental intervention will seek to become increasingly transversal to the different services and programmes, assuming itself as a condition and prior criterion of evaluation of the integrity of initiatives and projects. In fact, it's an important factor that distinguishes what qualifies as good practice both for individuals and institutions.

The severity of the environmental and climatic situation is a challenge to our intelligence and our will. The complexity of the issues and their reach in space and time challenge our categories of comprehension and invite many to succumb to an attitude of cynicism and resignation. On the other hand, the financial and economic crisis is seen by some as a factor that competes with the environmental and climatic concerns.

Both these two perspectives are wrong. Cynicism is corrected with the concrete experiences of individual and collective actions, demonstrating the plastic capacity that helps us to change direction. Part of contemporary culture is already sounding an alert in this tenacious fight against cynicism and nihilist disbelief. For example, the recent works by the 1988 Prix Goncourt winner Erik Orsenna, which he named *Petits précis de mondialisation* (*Voyage aux pays du coton* [2006] and *L'avenir de l'eau* [2008]), are informed and mobilising alerts.

The other error is the sign of great intellectual laziness. The economic crisis, instead of going against the change to a more sustainable society, can and should be understood as an opportunity to catalyse a profound and necessary change in models. That is what the best economists teach us, specifically, Sir Nicholas

Stern, whose latest essay, *A Blueprint for a Safer Planet*, was published in Portugal within the Gulbenkian Environment Collection under the title *Desafio Global*.

Blind belief in the potentials of science and technology is an escape from confronting the real problems. As Professor Filipe Duarte Santos says in his *Que Futuro? Ciência, Tecnologia, Desenvolvimento e Ambiente* (Gradiva, 2007), 'The ability of science and technology to assure continuity in the current paradigm of growth is limited, ultimately by the laws of nature. Despite Promethean convictions we don't have and will never have the ability to change the laws of nature. It is these that condition the future development of humanity.'

The changes that matter are technological and political, but also mental. They involve the complex software of the human spirit, where all the decisive wars are waged: understanding, confronting and acting.

To conclude, I would like to thank Sir David King who is going to present the inaugural paper of the Conference, and on his behalf I want to show my appreciation to all those who have agreed to contribute to these two days of reflection, underlining the important message that the President of the European Commission sent us. Finally, I would like to express my thanks to Professor Viriato Soromenho-Marques, who guarantees with his know-how and enthusiasm the coordination of the Gulbenkian Environment Programme and is responsible for the Conference's conception, as well as all the Foundation's team who contributed to making it happen.

In his poem *Leaves of Grass*, Walt Whitman claims to be terrified at the Earth, due to its serenity and patience, despite all the attacks it suffers at human hands.

Now I am terrified at the Earth, it is that calm and patient,

It grows such sweet things out of such corruptions, it turns harmless and stainless on its axis, with such endless successions of diseas'd corpses,

It distils such exquisite winds out of such infused fetor,

It renews with such unwitting looks its prodigal, annual,
sumptuous crops,

It gives such divine materials to men, and accepts such
leavings from them at last.

I believe that we shouldn't wait another century to see if the
Earth's apparent calm and patience, in the circumstance of a beautiful poem, should impose on us today another attitude of active
respect for the unique gift that is life on our planet.

Emílio Rui Vilar
October 2009

Translated by Janette Ramsay

Introduction
Environmental Crisis?
Do We Know What We Are
Talking About?

VIRIATO SOROMENHO-MARQUES

It was Ernest Gellner who coined the expression 'modular man' to define the fragmented state of the human condition in the different waves of modernity that we are submerged in. Each of us passes through different experiences, simultaneously carrying out different roles, not always carrying a logic or a unifying and coherent force.[1]

Contrary to what used to happen with the predictable inhabitants of pre-modern societies, or what continues to happen with those members of contemporary society marked by the homogeneity of historically buried fundamentalisms aggressively returned to the centre stage of history, we citizens of democratic societies from the West will not be fooled by clothing or eating habits. We are the holders of an enigma of our pluralism, prisoners of the capacity to carry out multiple functional roles or to articulate the most disconcerting of language games. From reflection on the exterior of our partial gestures and behaviours, no one can deduce or guess what we are as a whole. There may even be the suspicion that this whole is improbable, or a mere work in progress.

I would like to extend the 'modularity' hypothesis to the area of the environmental crisis, which since 2006 and 2007 has returned to the centre of worldwide political and media rhetoric, especially through the growing concerns regarding the evidence of climate change, and converging in the fragile consensus apparent among political, economic and social players concerning the severity of what is at risk in this process, as well as the urgency to make a response on the same scale as the threat. The Copenhagen Conference in December 2009 failed, despite previous hopes that, contrary to what happens so often, in this case of environmental and climate crises, the alerts and cautions of the scientific community would not fall onto the sterile soil of inertia among those in command but rather would become fertile humus that would feed the coming together of the international community in a common approach against the ontological danger that characterises this century. Is that what it is all about? Do we all mean the same thing when we talk about 'environmental crisis'? Or is it that, stuck in the functional dilacerations of our 'modularity', made up of disparate values, perspectives and interests, we reflect the environmental crisis as the light of the thousand sparks of a broken mirror, incapable of producing or sharing a common representation of this global threat?

1. Ambiguities in the 'Crisis' Concept

Words serve to differentiate mundane things and acts, to steer thought in the task of illuminating the paths where the action is projected and prolonged. When we talk about the environmental crisis, we run the risk of not adequately performing this task of identification of differences.

The crisis concept has been suffering, both in day-to-day language and academic discourse, a levelling process of losing the capacity to be a significant semantic vector. The word has suffered from overuse, being used to designate critical situations that go from mental health to the functioning of capital markets. It has become a buzzword, dominated by ambiguity.

There are two semantic segments contained in the origin of the word 'crisis', based on ancient Greek, that have been confused to the extent that a significant tension has been lost, which would result from their active maintenance and coexistence, as follows: the difference between *the act of judging* (such as a doctor's diagnosis or a judge's sentence) and *the act of deciding*, which brings us to the urgent need to overcome in word and deed the difficulties encountered in a path that has lost its way. It is in the poem by Parmenides (fragment 8.15) that these two primordial dimensions clearly emerge, with equal weight on both, judgement and decision.

In everyday language, the word 'crisis' has often been left in the narrow sphere of *judgement*. The crucial domain of *decision* has been forgotten, or, at least, put in a secondary position, being perceived more as something that results from the crisis and not as an intrinsic demand in comprehending it. And there's a world of difference between thinking of the decision as part of something, or as situated externally to it.

The semantic integrity of the crisis concept, in its original meaning, is of huge importance if we want to establish a sufficient understanding of what is going on at a global level with the state of the environment (and not just the climate that is certainly an essential configuration of the planetary ecosystem, globally considered). To call the situation a crisis will not be sufficient without understanding that the diagnosis of the environmental situation cannot be separated from adequate and timely decisions, that is to say, from all the necessary measures to face the threatening aspects identified in the diagnostic. These measures include political laws and strategies; research, scientific and technological innovation; financial investment and economic entrepreneurism; not to mention changes in individual behaviour and small-scale actions by individual citizens in their ethos as responsible consumers.

Sadly, academic discourse has also contributed to the weakening of the alert function contained in the concept behind the word crisis, thus weakening its role of anticipation of threats and dangers. Throughout the best of our intellectual tradition there has been a certain amount of appeasability, which varies between tragic pathos and epic exaltation, with the role of demiurge of the new and even of the alleged agent of progress, carried out by the crisis in modernity. The philosopher Hegel condenses this idea well when he proffers the famous declaration: 'Universal history is not the basis of happiness. In it happy periods are blank pages.'[2] How can we proclaim alerts or mobilise responses if crisis seems to be the driving force of historic destiny, of all that must be registered in the pungent chronicles of historic memory?

2. Between Crisis and Collapse

Periods of crisis are, really, exceptional moments in the history of peoples and individuals. They test creative capacities, the resistance and resilience of social groups, institutions and people. Based on our own experience, each of us can understand the truth in the aforementioned statement by Hegel. Nevertheless, 'overcoming' (*Aufhebung*) the more negative aspects of any crisis should not lead us to the extreme position of making banal the suffering, pain and destruction normally associated with it. The colossal injustices, loss of lives and dilapidation of the wealth achieved through human work that are committed in wars, revolutions or in the technological metamorphosis of the economic systems – critical moments par excellence – cannot be annulled and forgotten due to the positive result that the future may find in the final balance of these transformations. Contrary to the very disseminated court of history, what we can expect from it is not a sentence that forgives debts and absolves guilt, but the difficult and pitiful conservation of the empirical data, the chronicle of events, the most rigorous articulation of the facts, so that these may survive the successive waves of interpretation that each generation develops about the past, making it their own past, controlling it through hermeneutics that are always in a (re-)elaboration phase.

The idea that there's a limit beyond which the productivity of the crisis becomes materially impossible and morally unacceptable has been lost in the greater intellectual tendencies of modernity.

Optimism, especially technological or techno-centred optimism, has taken on a leading role in relation to other readings, both from the past and in relation to the task of evaluating the possibilities contained in the future. Optimism has become a kind of a priori of the transcendental grid of the reading of history. This optimism brings together the most disparate schools of thought: from the postmodern heralds of the twenty-first century to the followers of Marx's history philosophy, for whom 'humanity only gives itself tasks that it is in a condition to resolve'.[3]

A similar attitude, often associated in the practical sphere with technophiles of the technological fix, often naive, that there will always be a technical device to solve any problem, no matter how gigantic it is, contributed greatly to the processes of organised blindness that permitted the accumulation (almost lost in space and time) of the factors and indicators of the environmental crisis we now find ourselves in. It's not surprising, therefore, that it was about the environment that reflections from different sciences and schools of thought arose in search for a vision capable of returning to the concept of crisis its original sense of alert and urgency.

In 1949, Bertrand Russell posed a critical question: can our scientific society stabilise and survive its own expansion dynamics? The answer would depend on our ability to accommodate the disruptive dynamics caused by three critical factors of systemic impact: excessive demographic growth, risk of nuclear war and environmental aggression. For Russell, the cataclysmic hole left by the negative impact of economic growth on the ecosystems was evident: 'Both industry and agriculture, to a continually increasing degree, are carried on in ways that waste the world's capital of natural resources.'[4]

But how can we name a crisis that runs the risk of not revealing the most heroic fibre of individuals' and the institutions' capacity to perform well, but instead leading us to a desert of ruins, to the most abandoned silence that Earth has ever heard since it has been inhabited by men and women? What name do we give to an environmental crisis that appears to be more critical than any of the others that preceded it or that accompany it?

A good contribution to an answer to this essential question was given by the Canadian, Thomas Homer-Dixon, when he baptised our times as being characterised by an 'ingenuity gap'. Contrary to displaying the typical optimism of technophiles, Homer-Dixon advises us to look with prudence at our contemporary challenges, so great and complex are they. We're dealing with a kind of race against time, between threateningly real global problems (especially environmental ones) and their potential solutions, possible but still far from being effective. It's a race that has yet to be decided, but that, for the moment, seems more inclined towards the side of the current tortuous problems than the solutions that the future may hold for them.[5]

How can we name a crisis without a visible solution, a crisis that can dive into itself, into an implosion process with unexpected characteristics and consequences? There's no doubt that we can only answer this question with another concept, 'collapse'. Jared Diamond and other authors have quite rightly tried to draw attention to the special nature of an environmental crisis. A crisis that becomes a collapse cannot be absorbed by any 'optimistic' logic. The collapsed civilisations so attentively studied by Diamond on a global level, and with a historic amplitude that is often millennial, end up in ruins in silence. They are the victory of evil and of nothing over all the justifications and theodicy.[6]

At its most radical limit, the global environmental crisis that we all talk about could run the risk of being just the start of a global process that could drag human civilisation as a whole, for the first time in history, into an ontological abyss. A crisis that would really be the antechamber of the collapse. If the situation is so serious, how is it possible that we have not understood enough about it, generating the scientific and political consensus necessary to move to decisive action and the measures to avoid the rupture? How is it possible that the most advanced technological and scientific society that the planet has ever known runs the risk of arriving too late at the uncertain crossroads between a way of *crisis* and another way – that leads to *collapse*?

3. Is the Environmental Crisis a Proper Object of Scientific Enquiry?

Twentieth-century mass popular culture (the equivalent to, in a gross analogy, 'popular philosophy', eighteenth-century Prussian *Populärphilosophie*), which continues to impact, at least partially, throughout our twenty-first century, dominated a conception of science characterised by mixing elements of, on the one hand, positivist self-confidence ('only science has the conditions to produce real knowledge'), and on the other hand, our most ingenuous hopes ('science is the most noble and disinterested human activity, spontaneously aiming at humanity's well-being'). A similar model of popular belief and science, combining in the same crucible the search for truth and philanthropy, could only have been predicted as the main protection for us humans against all types of current or potential danger, and therefore as being the main candidate not just for the identification of the global environmental crisis but also the timely presentation of the most efficient measures to combat it efficiently, that is to say, in a preventive way.

But the difference between the ideal world of convictions that are part of the mythology of our mass media societies, and reality, couldn't be more different. If we consider the process of forming constitutive problems of what we could today call the *constellation of the environmental crisis*, what can be said, at least, is that as we do it we will be in a position to elaborate a type of gallery of heroes and heroines.

They are solitary voices, that, in most cases, encountered strong hostility or inhospitable indifference from their peers. Right from the start, Robert Malthus, father of the demographic alarm, saw his name transformed into an insult; as did Svante Arrhenius on climate change; Aldo Leopold on environmental ethics issues; Rachel Carson on the omnipresent chemical contamination of the food chain; Jacques-Yves Cousteau on the destruction of marine ecosystems; Kenneth Boulding on ecological economy; Hannah Arendt on the metaphysics of difficult times; to name but a few such pioneers.

The heroes and heroines in any area of human activity exist to be praised. Their sacrifice signals trails yet to be explored and their courage serves to feed the belief in us that perhaps the existence of humanity has not been in vain. Nevertheless, scientific heroism as a solitary experience is almost a contradiction in terms. What differentiates the pre-modern 'friend of knowledge' from the modern 'scientist' is the fact that the latter is part of one or various groups of researchers. For us, science is a precise institutional and methodological process, with standards and routines, a process with public spaces for constant dialogue and critical observation, comprising universities, institutes, academies, research centres, laboratories, scientific journals, conferences and seminars. It was Francis Bacon who first identified the idea of a scientific community – with an area for research but also for the presentation and validation of data and respective results – as being inseparable from the actual existence of science as an institution that would change humanity's direction forever.

It is extraordinary to affirm the asymmetry between what is monstrously and frighteningly at stake with the possibility of environmental collapse and the relative paucity of what has been effectively done by the scientific community to confront it. Let me take just two examples, in order not to shock you. First, although we have had literature on climate change, since at least the first essay written on the theme by Svante Arrhenius in 1896, the truth is that it was not until 1988 that the Intergovernmental Panel for Climate Change (IPCC) was established and only in the past three decades did significant investment in more profound studies and research on the climate begin. Secondly, despite the degree of general public awareness and the scientific information available on the great problems of the environmental constellation, from climate to biodiversity, from the oceans to the scarcity of fresh water or energy, the truth is that if we compare what societies invest in the study and protection of the environment with what is invested in military defence and in business as usual, it is impossible not to be stunned by the huge advantage of the latter.

It would be absurd and even counterproductive not to consider the environmental crisis as an object of scientific activity. It's important also to recognise that it only acquired this status late and with difficulty. And this fact, this late and unwilling integration of the environmental crisis into the objects of the *episteme*, was not due to any negligence, omission or forgetfulness, but rather it is inscribed in the matrix of modern science itself. Modern science was not born to cause social alarm, as Descartes stated, it was born to greatly increase material comforts and the healthy duration of human existence. Or, as Francis Bacon wrote, for 'the enlarging of the bounds of Human Empire, to the effecting of all things possible'.[7] Modern science appeared to bring us good news, to be transformed into the armed conqueror of utopia, bringing it from the future to the present, from heaven to earth, to make hedonism not a school of moral thought but a normal experience for the citizens of modern techno-scientific societies. The environmental crisis, to the contrary, talks of alarm and not of hope. It incites us to moderation and prudence, not to conquest and the glory that accompanies it. That's why it has arrived late as an object of study, due to the difficulty in entering in its own right into the modern city of science.

4. The Environmental Crisis in the Network of the Complexities of Scientific Endeavour

The only statement that can be made with absolute certainty regarding the integration of the environmental crisis into the scientific arena is that each step will be subject to powerful resistance, regardless of the area of the environmental constellation or the specialities that will be recruited for research. What we do know upfront is that if science takes on a critical attitude, then sounding alerts concerning established orders and regimes (be they legal or economic) will provoke a violent reaction, a disproportionate one, due to the conflict of interests. Two different examples from the past illustrate this statement. First, the aggressive campaign against Rachel Carson, promoted and financed by the chemical industry, irritated by the cry of alert against pesticides contained in the seminal work, *Silent Spring*. Secondly, the extremely strong attacks by the tobacco industry over decades against the public health professionals who denounced the lethal dangers involved in smoking tobacco, not just for active smokers but also for passive ones. Who is surprised that nowadays, even when the proofs and facts of climate change are clear and well-known, voices are raised proffering gross attacks against climate research and the scientists who most stand out due to their advice for prudence in public policy?

Nevertheless, it would be simplifying things to consider that the difficulties arising regarding scientific research on the environment come from outside science. In order to better understand the reasons that condition, limit and even prevent timely widespread consensus regarding important environmental issues, we would have to understand the web of complexities that, within the practice of science itself, ends up creating a considerable degree of opacity and entropy for progress in research and how this conveniently articulates with political orientations that should embrace the best scientific recommendations possible.

In my opinion, the following are the main complexities and obstacles:

4.1 Epistemological Complexity

Science is in general a difficult activity. It demands long academic preparation and uninterrupted training throughout one's life. Taking into account the personal sacrifices and the degree of dedication and discipline that this job demands, it is no accident that doing science is said to be not just a profession, but also rooted in a vocation. Most of the major environmental issues are by nature interdisciplinary; they demand combined effort from different areas of knowledge. The construction of heuristic approaches to establishing the collection of environmental data, as well as its analysis and interpretation, constitutes a huge epistemological challenge, especially if we consider the vertical structure of the different areas and the actual orientation of universities towards specialisation, at least at a graduate level and for those immediately above. Project leaders, faced with the difficulties raised by the epistemological complexity of environmental issues, will hesitate between going ahead or carrying out a more comfortable project within their speciality.

4.2 Organisational Complexity

To a much greater extent than was anticipated by Francis Bacon in the seventeenth century, a scientific project is nowadays a true company. Knowledge, methodological discipline and, if possible, a stroke of genius on the part of the researchers involved, is no longer enough. Company management skills are indispensable if projects wish to obtain financial resources in order to be able to properly fulfil their ambition. With the environment, and especially when we are dealing with global environmental problems, as is the case with climate change, this organisational complexity increases tremendously. In order to be able to feed, for example, the IPCC, working as a global network, multiple skills need to be combined, varying from accessing public and private funds – always scarce in more competitive areas – to the ability to be able to communicate to the public, not forgetting the urgent need to maintain constant supervision over the methodology that allows for quality control of the scientific contents themselves, so that mutual trust between researchers from various different areas will assure that there are no doubts regarding the credibility and reliability of the published results.

4.3 Complexity of Paradigms

The environmental crisis has been kept in the shade for decades, not because the symptoms were not visible in the real physical world but because the dominant points of view from the different areas of science kept them relatively invisible. It's all about the general functioning of scientific paradigms, so well explained by Thomas Kuhn in his classic work of 1962. The main obstacle to consensus in environmental sciences resides in the fact that the diagnosis of the environmental crisis questions the basic foundations of the dominant paradigms, and therefore the psychologically comfortable ones, foundations that, although they are based on belief and conviction, work as rules – although they don't have the same degree of legitimacy.[8] In fact, the basic axioms of a paradigm can be read, simultaneously, as windows and walls, as angles of vision but also as factors of opacity. To a great extent, some of the contemporary debates on the most critical areas of the global crisis cut through that, as participants know where the windows are and where they became walls preventing the penetration of light from the objective outside world.

4.4 Complexity of Expectations

Modern science was born under the sign of a demand for more power for humanity. The sought-after truth would not be a disinterested truth but a really useful one. As Descartes wrote in the *Discourse on the Method*, we should become 'masters and owners of Nature'. Scientific discourse and research, especially with the advent of the rapid secularisation of western societies and with the entry into a phase of decline of the great religious narratives, transformed themselves, for some time, into the only activity with some ability to produce credible discourses. It's not surprising that almost all the ideologies of the twentieth century, from bolshevism to racism, looked for a scientific basis for their delirious visions of the future. The advent of the environmental crisis, as a scientific theme, was to radically contradict this 'civil religion' vocation that science had achieved and sought to preserve. The experience of the environmental crisis, with its courting of technological catastrophes, identifies and underlines the contemporary rupture in the expectations of a technical euphoria bordering on magic. The sciences of the environmental crisis raise their voices, precisely during a phase when science itself is in a process of decline from its secular pedestal, and starting to be discussed in public places as if it were just one of many various opinions. This change, while it is not exempt from positive possibilities, contains the risk of ruining science's credibility, and of degrading its role in the contribution to public policy development and the production of confidence and social cohesion itself.[9]

5. Is a 'Back to Earth' Science Possible?

No one today is in a position to be able to respond with rigour to the fundamental ontological question of our time, which consists in knowing if our civilisation will be capable of evolving positively, facing the lethal challenges of the global environmental crisis, or, to the contrary, will become slow and hesitant, stuck in our inertia and conflicts, incapable of building working consensus, leaving us teetering above the abyss of collapse. What we can safely say now is that for the first possibility to succeed we will have to count on an even more intense involvement of science and the scientific community in all of its dimensions, in the construction of the conditions that will allow us to traverse the dangerous era of transition we have already embarked on.

In my opinion, there are two essential conditions that must be fulfilled should science want to play this decisive role in the risky, current transition of civilisation. The first condition has been well summarised by Bob Doppelt when he alerted us to the urgent task of rearranging the relationship between knowledge and subjects, so as to be ready for climate change.[10] Doppelt's appeal deals with the new responsibilities of social sciences, including, obviously, economics and sociology among others. Continuing to insist on the treatment of climate change, as the most visible part of the environmental crisis, merely under the scope of physical and natural sciences, would be a big mistake, would end up paralysing us in adequate and timely inspirational public policy planning. Much of the reverberating criticism of the IPCC raised by the media, especially in generalist media, derives from this lack of understanding of the need to widen the understanding of the environmental and climatic theme, leaving the shores of obsolete conceptions of certainty that make us run the risk of not seeing the difference between prediction and projection or between fact and trend, dragging science to a level of distrust, uselessness and paralysis.

The second condition is even more demanding and radical. Hannah Arendt best clarifies it in a 1963 text dedicated to the consequences, for our anthropologic identity, of the 'conquest of space'.[11] For most of us nowadays, when we look to the future and see increasingly thick and dominating clouds, it would seem prudent to drum into science's attitudes an aggressive and profound 'return to Earth'. After centuries of successive Copernican revolutions, of distancing, decentring and indifference in relation to our planet and the future of our species, what we need today is a kind of neo-Ptolomaic turnaround of knowledge, not in the sense of its substance (which would be absurd), but in terms of form. That is, it's about placing science at the service of human interest, which implies a combination of the two tasks. First, the intransigent defence of the Earth as a place where humans can live in dignified conditions. Secondly, the recognition of human fragility and mortality as inherent to our ability to give direction and meaning to an existence that can and deserves to be lived.

Translated by Janette Ramsay

Notes

1 Ernest Gellner, *Conditions of Liberty: Civil Society and its Rivals* (London: Alan Lane, 1994), pp. 97ff.

2 'Die Weltgeschichte ist nicht der Boden des Glücks. Die Perioden des Glücks sind leere Blätter in ihr', in G.W.F. Hegel, *Vorlesungen Über die Philosophie der Geschichte, Werke* (Frankfurt am Main: Suhrkamp, 1986), vol.12, p. 42.

3 '...*stellt sich die Menschheit nur Aufgaben, die sie lösen kann.*' Karl Marx, '*Vorwort zur Kritik der politischen Ökonomie* [1859]', in Günter Heyden and Anatoli Jegorow (eds), *Marx–Engels Gesamtausgabe* (Berlin: Dietz Verlag, 1980), vol. 2.2, p. 101. Seee also my text: 'O Desafio da Pós-Humanidade', in *Metamorfoses. Entre o Colapso e o Desenvolvimento Sustentável* (Mem Martins: Publicações Europa-América, 2005), pp. 183ff.

4 Bertrand Russell, 'Can a Scientific Society be Stable?', *British Medical Journal*, 10 December 1949, p. 1307.

5 Thomas Homer-Dixon, 'We are indeed in a race between hard imaginative thinking – or what I call ingenuity – and the ever expanding complications of our world. And in too many critical places, and on too many critical issues we're losing the race.' Thomas Homer-Dixon, 'Ingenuity Theory: Can Humankind Create a Sustainable Civilization?' 2003. See http://www.homerdixon.com/ingenuitygap/home.html.

6 Jared Diamond, *Collapse: How Societies Choose to Fail or Succeed* (New York: Penguin, 2004).

7 Francis Bacon, *New Atlantis and the Great Instauration*, ed. Jerry

Weinberger (Arlington Heights, IL: Harlan Davidson, 1989), p. 71.

8 'Rules, I suggest, derive from paradigms, but paradigms can guide research even in the absence of rules.' Thomas S. Kuhn, *The Structure of Scientific Revolutions* [1962], in *International Encyclopaedia of Unified Science* (Chicago: University of Chicago Press), vol. 2.2, p. 42.

9 The problem of communication in science is one of the fundamental themes of the theory of 'post-normal science' developed by Jerome Ravetz and Sílvio Funtowicz. See, e.g., J. Ravetz, 'When Communication Fails: A Study of Failures of Global Systems', in Ângela G. Pereira, Sofia G. Vaz and Sylvia Tognetti (eds), *Interfaces Between Science and Society* (Sheffield: Greenleaf, 2006), pp. 16–34.

10 'One of the problems is that the issue is still being framed as a scientific and environmental issue. This is a major mistake. Climate change is just a symptom of dysfunctional social and economic practices and policies. It is a social and economic issue. The emphasis needs to shift away from the biophysical sciences now to the social sciences if we have any hope of solving this problem.' Bob Doppelt, *Guardian*, 14 April 2009.

11 'It would be geocentric [the new science] in the sense that the earth, and not the universe, is the centre and the home of mortal men, and it would be anthropomorphic in the sense that man would count his own factual mortality among the elementary conditions under which his scientific efforts are possible at all.' Hannah Arendt, 'The Conquest of Space and the Stature of Man' [1963], in *Between Past and Future: Eight Exercises in Political Thought* (New York: Penguin, 1993), pp. 265–80.

Notes on Contributors

Emílio Rui Vilar

Emílio Rui Vilar was born in Oporto in 1939. He graduated in Law from Coimbra University (1961). Since May 2002, he has been President of the Board of Trustees of the Calouste Gulbenkian Foundation and Chairman of the Board of Directors of Partex Oil and Gas (Holdings) Corporation. Throughout his life, Emílio Rui Vilar has held many distinguished positions and is currently the President of the Portuguese Foundation Centre, Chairman of the European Foundation Centre and Co-President of the Global Philanthropy Institute.

He has been a Guest Professor at the School of Economics and Management of the Portuguese Catholic University since 1998. Emílio Rui Vilar was Chairman of the Audit Commission, Banco de Portugal (1996), and from 1989 to 1996 Chairman and CEO of the Caixa Geral de Depósitos (National Savings Bank). He served as General Commissioner of Europalia Portugal (1989–92); Director General of the European Committee Commission (1986–89); and Deputy Governor of the Banco de Portugal (1975–84). In Government, he has served as Minister of Transport and

Communications (1976–78); Minister of the Economy (1974–75); and as Secretary of State for External Trade and Tourism (1974).

Viriato Soromenho-Marques

Viriato Soromenho-Marques (born 1957) teaches Political Philosophy and European Ideas in the Departments of Philosophy and European Studies of the University of Lisbon. He is the scientific coordinator of the Environment Programme of the Calouste Gulbenkian Foundation; member of the President of the European Commission's Advisory Group on Energy and Climate Change; and a member of the Lisbon Academy of Sciences. Since 1978 he has been engaged in the civic environmental movement in Portugal and Europe. He has been a member of the National Council on Environment and Sustainable Development since 1998. He was Vice-Chair of the European Environmental and Sustainable Development Advisory Councils Network from 2001 to 2006, and co-authored the Portuguese National Strategy for Sustainable Development (2004). More information regarding his extensive bibliography and activities may be found at his Web site, www.viriatosoromenho-marques.com.

David King

Sir David King is the Director of the Smith School of Enterprise and Environment at the University of Oxford. He was the UK Government's Chief Scientific Advisor and Head of the Government Office of Science from 2000 to 2007 and is also Director of Research in Physical Chemistry at Cambridge University. Sir David is President of the British Science Association; President of the Collegio Carlo Alberto, Turin, Italy; Advisor to President Kagame of Rwanda; Advisor on African Development to the European Commissioners; and Senior Science Advisor to UBS.

Miguel Bastos Araújo

Miguel Bastos Araújo holds the Rui Nabeiro Chair of Biodiversity at the University of Évora, Portugal, and is a senior researcher at the Spanish Research Council. Professor Araújo is also a senior research associate of the Oxford University Centre for the

Environment, an international collaborator with the Copenhagen University Centre for Macroecology, and a member of the International Laboratory on Global Change. Professor Araújo serves as deputy editor-in-chief of *Ecography*, associate editor of the *Journal of Biogeography, Conservation Letters, Geography Compass*, and is a member of the scientific committee of DIVERSITAS's bioDISCOVERY programme. He contributed to the 2007 Fourth IPCC (Intergovernmental Panel for Climate Change) Assessment Report, for which the IPCC shared the Nobel Peace Prize.

Pedro Arrojo Agudo

Pedro Arrojo Agudo holds a PhD in Physical Sciences from the University of Zaragoza and is now a Professor in the University's Economic Analysis Department. Over the past 20 years, his research has focused on the Economics of Water. Pedro Arrojo Agudo was Chairman of the first two Iberian Congresses on Water Planning and Management and Chairman of the First Latin American Meeting for a New Water Culture. Between 2001 and 2003, he led the interdisciplinary team of the Fundación Nueva Cultura del Agua, which assisted the European Commission during the debate on the Spanish National Water Plan. In 2005, he chaired the Scientific Committee that drew up the European Declaration for a New Water Culture. In 2006, he took part in the Spanish Ministry of the Environment's Expert Committee on Drought Management and, in 2007, he chaired the Ministry's Expert Committee on Water Markets. Pedro Arrojo is a member of the Water Council of the Ebro Basin; member of the UNESCO Man and the Biosphere (MAB) Committee; and a member of the Scientific Committee of the World Congress of the International Water Resources Association (IWRA, Madrid 2003). Until 2010, he chaired the Fundación Nueva Cultura del Agua, which organised the Iberian Congresses on Water Planning and Management. In 2003, he was awarded in San Francisco the Goldman Environmental Prize for Europe.

José Lima Santos

José Lima Santos is Professor at the Institute of Agronomy,

Technical University of Lisbon, and Head of the Department of Agricultural Economics and Rural Sociology at the same Institute. His main research and teaching areas are Environmental Economics, the Economic Valuation of the Environment, Cost–Benefit Analysis of Public Policy, Policy Analysis, and Agri-environment Policy Design and Evaluation.

José Lima Santos has worked as an expert for the OECD in a number of roles, including the Economic Valuation of Biodiversity (1998/9) and the Multifunctionality of Agriculture (Washington workshop, 2000). Between 2000 and 2003 he was Director-General of the Agri-Food Planning and Policy Bureau, Ministry of Agriculture. He helped coordinate policy negotiations towards the 2003 Common Agricultural Policy (CAP) reform. José Lima Santos has been a member of the National Environment and Sustainable Development Council (CNADS) since 2006, and a member of the Consultative Committee of the Gulbenkian Environmental Programme since 2007.

Gilles Lipovetsky

Born in France in 1944, Gilles Lipovetsky is Associate Professor of Philosophy at the University of Grenoble. As an essayist, he analyses how regulations, values and behaviours evolve in the European developed societies. He holds Honorary Doctorates from the University of Sherbrooke (Canada) and New Bulgarian University (Sofia). He is a member of two advisory bodies to the French Government, the Ministry of National Education's National Programmes Council and the Conseil d'Analyse de la Société (CAS), and a consultant with the association, Progrès du Management. Gilles Lipovetsky was awarded France's highest honour, Knight of the Légion d'Honneur. He has published an extensive bibliography that is translated or being translated in 18 countries.

Allan Larsson

Born in 1938, Allan Larsson forged a professional career in print and television journalism, economic research, national politics and in public administration in Sweden and the European Union. In

2007, he was appointed Chief Negotiator in Sweden's bid to host the ESS, a European multidisciplinary science facility. He is Chairman of the University of Lund; a member of the Advisory Committee on Leadership, Governance and Management of the Higher Education Funding Council for England; member of the Royal Swedish Academy of Engineering Sciences; member of President Barroso's High Level Group on Energy and Climate Change; and Member of the Jacques Delors' Notre Europe Steering Committee.

In Government, he served as Undersecretary of State at the Ministry of Labour (1974–76); Director General of the National Labour Market Board (1983–90); Minister of Finance (1990) and as an elected member of the Swedish Parliament (1991). He was a member of the Board of Governors of the Central Bank (1992–94). Allan Larsson has served as Chairman of the European Employment Initiative; Director-General of the European Commission in Brussels, responsible for employment and social affairs; and from 1995 to 2000, oversaw preparation and implementation of the European Employment Strategy. In 2001, he joined Kofi Annan's High Level Panel on Youth Employment.

He was Chairman of the Board of Swedish Television and Chairman of the Transatlantic Dialogue on Broadcasting and the Information Society. He was also a member of the OECD Round Table on Sustainable Development in Paris (2001–2003) and personal representative of Director General Juan Somavia, ILO, to the Johannesburg Summit on Sustainable Development. From 2005 to 2008, he was a member of the Albright–de Soto Commission for Legal Empowerment of the Poor.

Malini Mehra
Malini Mehra is the founder and CEO of the Centre for Social Markets, a non-profit organisation that has pioneered work on sustainability and corporate responsibility in India and its Diaspora. In 2007, CSM launched Climate Challenge India, the country's first national mobilisation campaign on climate change promoting a fiercely proactive, leadership agenda. She has published widely on these issues and is a frequent media commentator. In 2009, she was

named a Young Global Leader by the World Economic Forum; in 2007, an Asia 21 Young Leader by the Asia Society; and in 2006 she was chosen as a Principal Voice by CNN. Prior to founding CSM in 2000, Malini worked on international trade, environment and human rights for NGOs including Oxfam and Friends of the Earth. From 2005 to 2006, she served at the UK government, where she led on international sustainable development partnerships and initiated the UK's Sustainable Development Dialogues (SDDs) with China, India, Brazil, South Africa and Mexico. From 2004 to 2005, she served as advisor to UN Secretary-General Kofi Annan on his High Level Panel of Eminent Persons on UN–Civil Society Relations. She has also contributed to UN publications such as the Human Development Reports on Democracy (2002) and Human Rights (2000) respectively.

Pedro Martins Barata
Pedro Martins Barata is currently a member of the Executive Board of the Clean Development Mechanism. He is a consultant to the Ministry of Environment in Portugal on climate issues, acting as Senior Policy Officer for the Interministerial Climate Change Commission. He has worked on the Portuguese delegation to the climate change talks since 1999 and chaired the EU Expert Group on Carbon Market Mechanisms during the Portuguese EU presidencies of 2000 and 2007 and the Slovenian presidency of 2008. He has been a consultant to the European Commission and to international environmental NGOs on international environmental policy issues. He was Vice-President of Quercus, the largest environmental NGO in Portugal (1999–2001), and served on the Board of the European Environmental Bureau as Portuguese representative. He holds an MSc in environmental economics and policy from the LSE and is currently a PhD candidate at Lisbon University, with a thesis on environmental and climate impact assessment of energy subsidies in Spain and Portugal.

Julie Packard
In the late 1970s, Julie helped found the Monterey Bay Aquarium and has served as the Aquarium's Executive Director since its

opening. In its twentieth year the Aquarium launched the Centre for the Future of the Oceans, the goal of which is to protect the oceans by promoting sound conservation policy.

Julie has served as a trustee of the David and Lucile Packard Foundation for 34 years and has been deeply involved in the Foundation's Conservation and Science Programmes. She also chairs the Board of the Monterey Bay Aquarium Research Institute, dedicated to the development of new technologies for understanding the deep sea and global ocean systems. She has served on numerous other boards and committees related to conservation, including the California Nature Conservancy and World Wildlife Fund. She was the 1998 recipient of the Audubon Medal for Conservation; of the 2004 Ted Danson Ocean Hero Award from Oceana, a leading ocean conservation organisation; was elected in 2009 as a Fellow of the American Academy of Arts and Sciences, and was named a California Coastal Hero in 2009 by the California Coastal Commission and *Sunset* magazine. Julie was a member of the Pew Oceans Commission, a diverse group of US leaders charged with developing recommendations to improve ocean resource management.

Nitin Desai

Nitin Desai, a graduate of the LSE, taught economics at two UK universities, worked briefly in the private sector, had a long stint as a government official in India and later in the UN where he was Under-Secretary-General for Economic and Social Affairs at his retirement in 2003. His major work in the UN was the organisation of a series of global summits, including the Rio Earth Summit (1992) and the Johannesburg Sustainable Development Summit (2002). He is at present a member of the National Security Advisory Board and the Prime Minister's Council on Climate Change in India and remains an active participant in the national and global dialogue on climate policy.

Alex Ellis

Alexander Ellis has been the British Ambassador to Portugal since September 2007. Between 2005 and 2007 he was an advisor to the

President of the European Commission on energy, climate change, competition, development, trade and strategy. Prior to that, he worked on EU and economic issues in Madrid in the British Embassy; in London, as head of the Foreign Office's team for the negotiations for the 2004 EU enlargement, as well as EU–Turkey relations; in Brussels, in the UK Representation to the EU, working on the negotiations to establish the euro, the seven-year budget, then institutional issues including the Treaty of Nice; and in Lisbon, as a junior member of the political team in the British Embassy. He started his Foreign Office career as part of the team supporting the transition to multiparty democracy in South Africa, following the release of Nelson Mandela.

Miranda Schreurs

Miranda Schreurs is Director of the Environmental Policy Research Centre, Professor of Comparative Politics at the Freie Universität Berlin, and member of the German Environment Advisory Council. Prior to this she was Associate Professor in the Department of Government and Politics, University of Maryland. Her work focuses on comparative environmental and energy politics and policy. She was born and raised in the USA and has also lived for extended periods in Japan and briefly in the Netherlands prior to moving to Germany in 2007. Her PhD (1996) is from the University of Michigan and her MA and BA from the University of Washington. She has held fellowships from the SSRC-MacArthur Foundation Programme on International Peace and Security Affairs, the Fulbright Foundation (Japan and Germany), and the National Science Foundation/Japan Society for the Promotion of Science. She is currently Fulbright Distinguished Scholar Leader of the New Century Scholar's Programme, The University as Innovation Driver and Knowledge Centre.

Jonathon Porritt

Jonathon Porritt is Founder Director of Forum for the Future. He is an eminent writer, broadcaster and commentator on sustainable development. Established in 1996, Forum for the Future is now the UK's leading sustainable development charity, with 70 staff and over 100 partner organisations, including some of the world's leading companies.

Jonathon was Chairman of the UK Sustainable Development Commission between 2000 and 2009, the Government's principal source of independent advice across the whole sustainable development agenda. In addition, he is Co-Director of the Prince of Wales's Business and Environment Programme, which runs Senior Executives' Seminars in Cambridge, Salzburg, South Africa and the USA. In 2005 he became a Non-Executive Director of Wessex Water, and a Trustee of the Ashden Awards for Sustainable Energy, and in 2008 a Non-Executive Director of Willmott Dixon Ltd.

He was formerly Director of Friends of the Earth (1984–90); Co-chair of the Green Party (1980–83), of which he is still a member; Chairman of UNED-UK (1993–96); Chairman of Sustainability South West, the South West Round Table for Sustainable Development (1999–2001); a Trustee of WWF UK (1991–2005), and a member of the Board of the South West Regional Development Agency (1999–2008). Jonathon received a CBE in January 2000 for services to environmental protection.

Climate Change as a
Global Shifting Force

DAVID KING

I think after the previous presentation from Professor Viriato Soromenho-Marques I ought to explain that I am a scientist; I am a chemical physicist by training and also by practice for over 35 years. In addition, I went into Government, and was in Government for seven and a half years. There, I experienced science policy delivery, and after that, I left to join Oxford University to establish something that is totally new within a university – a School of Enterprise and the Environment. The School has achieved a great deal in the short time since then, including our first world forum last summer.

What the School is trying to do is to pull together experts from a range of academic disciplines. I have 60 professors from the university working with me, ranging from experts in engineering to political scientists to philosophers. We have 30 cross-disciplinary staff working full-time at the School and we are working with the private sector and governments around the world to find solutions to the problems that I am going to talk about.

The idea behind the Smith School is not that we can manage all of this from within Oxford, but instead to create similar hubs in other parts of the world, and I am very pleased to say that we are fast establishing three or four of those.

I want to explain what I consider to be the missing role of science in the policy regime by referring to some work that is unrelated to climate change but nevertheless is environmental in its impact, and this is the work of the people who study seismology and volcanology and who understand how the great plates carrying our continents are in constant movement around the planet.

About twenty years ago, these people set up a warning about where the next great disasters would be, based on their under-standing of where the plates were about to collide and cause sudden transitions. They pointed out that the next great disaster was going to be along the Sumatran trench. Then, in the summer of 2004, scientists from Oxford and California visited Indonesia, Sri Lanka and India to try to persuade the governments of those coun-tries to set up an early warning system in the Indian Ocean. They didn't manage to do this. Thirty million dollars would have been the cost.

Now, as you know, I am referring to the fact that the disaster they predicted along the Sumatran trench happened. They predicted a force nine tsunami and that is what happened. It took place on 26 December 2004 and 230,000 people lost their lives. How many would have been saved with an earlier warning system in place? My estimate is that 150,000 to 180,000 lives could have been saved with an early warning system in place. What are we doing now? We are now putting in place an early warning system in the Indian Ocean.

The classic response has been repeated again and again: we wait for a massive disaster and then we close the door after the horse has bolted. I refer to the Peruvian tsunami, again a force nine, that occurred in 1985. Again, the seismologists had said this was going to be the next big disaster, but very little attention was given to their warnings, to what the state of knowledge is currently with respect to these situations, because we have not, I would suggest, got the right connectivity between the knowledge base – the real understanding of what is happening – and the decision-making processes – and that is really what I was doing in the British

Government, trying to make that connection. But this was not only from a British Government point of view. I was also trying to work on a global scale, using our state of knowledge, not just from the sciences, but bringing together science with economics and our understanding of human behaviour, to see if we can better manage risk to our societies.

Now, of course, I shall address a set of situations where we cannot afford to wait until after the disaster. What I want to start with is the very good news. As we moved through the twentieth century, we saw a massive improvement in human well-being. We began the twentieth century with a life expectancy in many, many countries around the world of 40 to 45, and we ended the century with a life expectancy of around 80. Interestingly, life expectancy is still rising linearly with time in many of our countries. So, we nearly doubled life expectancy and if I can use just that as a crude measure of human well-being, then we can congratulate ourselves; I say, didn't we do well!

However, I suggest that this was delivered initially and very largely through civil engineering – the spread of clean water. Sanitary conditions around the world were an absolutely critical part of that increase, as were advances in medicine, agriculture, science and technology generally, coupled to the improvement of our social and political systems.

If we were to look at a map of the world in terms of life expectancy, we would see that my figure of 80 years actually applies to a relatively small part of the world. However, life expectancy is rising as we go around the world. If we look at India today, it is over 60, for that very large population. If we look at China, it is over 65; and these numbers are increasing year on year. But in the middle of our map we would see the part of the world I come from, Africa. In Africa life expectancy is still 45 or less, and 40 or less in many parts. So, there's the missing continent, and I wouldn't want this Conference to pass without noting that we have a piece of the world that has missed the benefits of the twentieth century.

Nevertheless, let's take the positive: life expectancy massively increased. But there is a negative side to that, because we entered the twentieth century with 5 billion people and then our life expectancy increased. That means the population dynamics are very simple and what follows, nation by nation, is that as more people live to maturity, they too have children and the population explodes. As we improved our life expectancy, we should have anticipated the follow through, which was a population explosion.

On average, in Britain in the Middle Ages, a woman had seven or eight children in her lifetime, of whom only two survived into maturity. So we had a relatively stable population over time. Then along came the civil engineers and women were caught out; they had a surprise for them: all seven or eight children survived into maturity.

There's the first factor in the sudden explosion of population. That appears to happen for about two generations, and then the culture shifts, female fecundity collapses, and we all know that this is happening in every country in Europe. It is happening in South America, too, where female fecundity has collapsed more recently than in any other area, from 6 children, 30 years ago, to 2.2. Now, throughout South America, it is 2.2.

So we see that population dynamics change with the intervention of female education, women in Parliament and the availability of contraceptives. I'm not saying that men have got nothing to do with this, just that we are pretty hopeless at it. But as we go through, we see it's self-limiting.

So the good message is that the population will not continue to rise forever. The medium expectation is that we will reach a population of 9 billion by mid-century and the population may even begin to decrease after that because average female fecundity is dropping below the magic figure of 2.1, which helps stabilise the population.

I am going to suggest that because the human population rose by a billion every 12 years in the twentieth century and reached 6 billion by the end of that century (we're now at 6.7), in 2028 we'll pass the 8 billion mark. We need to plan for a population of 9 billion people and not only expect a linear rise in consumption by those people, but a rising expectancy of consumption, because we are also seeing that wealth creation in the developing world is catching up with us.

So consumption is growing faster than the growth in the population. That is what we have to manage in the twenty-first century; and I want to suggest that we need a complete cultural rethink. We cannot simply extrapolate linearly from our behaviour in the twentieth century into the twenty-first because we have a hangover from that century represented by the population of 9 billion. Let's take a look at this figure, which is coming to be known as King's Carousel.

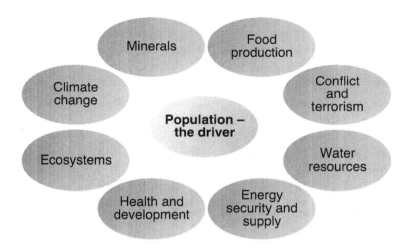

Figure 1. Twenty-first-century challenges

I suggest that we take population as the driver – and that is not a passive statement; let's do what we can, especially with female education and getting women into Parliament, but let's take population as the driver – then order some of the big challenges. Here I am selecting what I consider to be some of the biggest challenges around this carousel.

If only each of these challenges could be dealt with alone, then we could be reasonably optimistic. But I am suggesting that this is what physicists would call a many-body problem; it's a totally interactive system. So, if I can take one of the issues almost at random – water resources. If we look globally at water resources – I'm now talking about fresh water, although oceans are another aspect delivering a very big part of our ecosystem services – but if we just take fresh water supplies, as our population grows, we contaminate water. It is in our nature to provide sanitary conditions and therefore, as the population grows, the amount of fresh water available becomes less and less because the overall demand for water supply per head is roughly constant as we move forward in time.

When do we reach the point at which demand for fresh water globally exactly matches the supply? The answer is about 2040. That is only three decades away. That's the global situation and, of course, what we are seeing already is that in many places locally, with the warming crisis, there is a shortage of available water.

I give you an example taken not from the developing world – we can easily do that – but an example taken from the developed world. In the state of Victoria, South Australia, climate change has had an impact in two areas. Victoria has seen seven, eight and now nine successive years of drought. The farmers are literally giving up, yet this was a state that produced vegetables for a big part of the Australian continent. However, the state today is producing one-third of its fresh water for the whole state of Victoria, including the city of Melbourne and all the other towns and villages, from desalination. 'Desalination?' you say, 'Dave King is a scientist and a technologist and must be a happy man to see this…' Far from it. Desalination is an energy-intensive process, so we move around the circle of the carousel to energy security and supply.

Australia has plenty of coal, so Australia burns coal to desalinate water. But hold on, go across to climate change and burning coal produces CO_2. This causes global warming, but global warming worsens the problem we are trying to tackle, which is desertification. And there's the problem: *we get local solutions to a problem that don't actually fit into solutions for the global problems we need to tackle.*

So, we move forward in time, and I want to suggest that I could randomly choose any example from around the carousel as the missing parameter, such as ecosystems services. We coevolved with the planetary system over billions of years and humanity emerged in the period when we had this coequal agreement between vegetation and mammals, vegetation consuming carbon dioxide, mammals giving CO_2 and coevolving with the states of the oceans and so on; we had a rough equilibrium of gases in our atmosphere, which happened to be perfect for human beings.

Those ecosystem services are vast, and we utterly depend on them. Let me give you a historical example of a nation that ignored the ecosystem services and had to move on, and that is the Han People of China. That dynasty arose up in the Loess Plateau. The Han nation grew, became all powerful and began to overuse its territory, which became totally desertified as their farming practices did not recognise the ecosystem services that were being provided. So what the Emperor did in 1420 was simply to move the capital from the Loess Plateau to Beijing and most of his people followed. There was room in China to move the Han people to another area where, having learnt lessons from desertification, they began different practices. And the Mother River of the Loess Plateau, mother of the Han people, became known as the Yellow River, as the desert sands coloured the water. That is an example of where a whole people was unaware of what the ecosystems were delivering for them and therefore didn't protect them, but there was a chance to survive by moving elsewhere.

I suggest that with 9 billion people on this planet that is no longer an option. If we refer to the exponential growth models of economists, we have got round to ploughing the last furrow and therefore we need to manage our ecosystems as part of this global system in a way that we have not managed in the past.

Take food production. We are becoming a civilisation that consumes more and more meat. Because of that, we are almost paradoxically having to produce more crops as we move forward in time, and so, in 20 years' time it is likely that we will have to produce 50 per cent more food crops than we're producing at the moment to meet the rising demand of this rising population: 50 per cent more crops from which bits of land? Remember the population footprint is itself expanding.

We want to protect the ecosystem services otherwise we are not going to manage that process. So *we need to use the best that* science and technology can deliver into agricultural practice to meet that 50 per cent extra demand.

Why do I think we can succeed in that? Let me refer back to the debate in the 1960s about whether or not India could feed its population. There was a massive belief that India would never be able to feed its growing population. India can and does, and so does China, so does Malaysia; and the reason is that biotechnology benefited agricultural practice, the region developed and production rose sevenfold per hectare in those parts of the world.

So what we can see is that good practices can bring about the results we want. However, the question then is whether we are managing the process of switching to good practice and whether we are able to do this fast enough. Remember that I am suggesting we have only 20 years to increase food production so again we need a green revolution of the kind we have seen before to meet the demands. We need to act quite quickly, but as we do that, let's not do it by risking all these other factors around the carousel. One of the issues is getting 'more crop per drop', because, as I said, we have diminishing water resources. We need technology that delivers water directly to the plants that need it, rather than flooding the whole area. We know that technology is coming along. Now we need technology to produce crops that are drought-resistant for some areas and flood-resistant for other areas and disease-resistant too; we need the crop technologies to come along to manage these processes.

Things can go wrong when we act to deal with a single problem. Let me give as an example the sudden and very substantial rise in rice prices in 2008. From the beginning of 2008, rice prices rose by a factor of three, close to four. For most of us in the developed world this problem was barely noticeable, but I need to remind you that the bottom billion people in the world earn less than a dollar a day and are close to starvation and certainly suffered from malnutrition when the rice price went up.

So it is important that we analyse what is the cause or what are the causes, the major causes, of this particular event, which has had massive ramifications around the world. Through our analysis at the Smith School I set up in Oxford, we can now provide some numbers. We believe that 70 per cent of the price rise, plus or minus 10 per cent, is due to the US policy of subsidising farmers who turn corn as a food crop into a fuel crop to make alcohol. That alcohol can be turned into gasoline to reduce the dependence of the USA on imports of gasoline.

I am suggesting that those subsidies have nothing to do with climate change policy and everything to do with subsidising farmers and reducing the cost of importing gasoline. As a matter of fact, the carbon footprint of this process is not good at all, so it does not do much good for climate change. It is about 80 or 90 per cent of the carbon footprint of gasoline. So why do we attribute 70 per cent responsibility in our figures? Quite simply, because the excess food produced annually in the USA goes on to the world market, and when that is shut down, the world market sees a big rise in prices. This, I suspect, is an unintended consequence of a policy decision taken by one country.

The other 30 per cent is an effect that is with us annually, which is water-related. Farmers plant rice in paddy fields. Everyone knows that paddy fields are places where you can have a lot of water and the rice plant indeed needs a lot of water to fully ripen and grow and develop into a marketable product. But the problem arises that you're planting rice where there's a lot of water and if you plant your rice too early, the little rice plant draws in the water. The emerging rice plant cannot survive in a paddy field that is immersed in water for more than three days when the monsoon comes. So every year around the world, there is a large loss of the rice harvest, due to early flooding. And when there are early monsoons, there is an excessive loss of rice. I suggest that that too is an avoidable problem.

In India, in 1992, it was discovered that there is a wild rice variety that can survive flooding. That wild rice variety is not marketable; it produces rice but it is not a marketable product. Immediately, the biotechnology industry set about finding out which genes give the plant its flood resistance. By using genetic markers we quickly discovered which genes were responsible. The next step is to snip those genes into a marketable rice and create a flood-resistant rice which is then capable of being taken to the marketplace. But this rice has not reached the marketplace. Instead, in the International

Rice Research Institute in the Philippines, the same plant is being developed using genetic markers to help the process, but also using standard plant-breeding techniques with people in the mud up to their knees and elbows relying on annual development. So it's a very slow process.

We are very much hoping that this rice, capable of withstanding flooding for three weeks, will reach the marketplace next year. How many people have died each year, because that technology did not reach the marketplace sooner?

I suggest that with the snipping process I referred to, that rice could have been delivered by 1996 or 1997; yet we are now in 2010 and the number of people who have died of malnutrition or starvation during that process is massive.

Here is the interface with the social political system. In Europe, we have made what I consider to be a lifestyle choice against the process I have described. I've been avoiding using the term GMOs. We have said, give me a choice between a standard tomato and a tomato developed by this snipping process and I'll have the standard one, that's what I'm used to.

If you're starving in Africa, you don't have that choice, and yet, in Africa GMOs have been banned. Why have they been banned? Because they think if it's not good enough for Europeans, it can't be good enough for us. So we must remember that we make social decisions, which get exported to places where those decisions are actually very, very poor indeed in the local situation.

I am going to suggest that due to our opposition to GMOs, hundreds of thousands of people have lost their lives, yet there is no evidence of any single person suffering from eating a genetically modified food or foodstuff that has been regulated. Governments need to provide good regulatory behaviour that at least keeps in step with scientific advances.

To underline this point, let me remind you what the origins of modern corn are. In an entirely 'natural' state, the fully mature corn plant resembles grass. We have genetically modified it to produce this long cob and that feeds a significant part of the world. We have in our civilisation relied heavily on modifying plant behaviour to suit our needs and purposes.

Now, I'm suggesting in my title, and this follows on precisely from what we said before, that with this carousel of challenges, the driving force is coming from climate change, and the reason is, I think, relatively simple. Climate change, of all of these problems, is one we cannot solve one nation at a time. It is a problem that requires the collective response of all nations. It is qualitatively different from the problems we have been facing previously over the last hundred years. Here, we have got a problem that requires global agreement. Why? Because if one nation decides to stand aside from pricing CO_2, that nation becomes the manufacturing source of high-carbon products, so the problem isn't solved. This, I believe, is the biggest problem our civilisation has ever had to face up to, precisely because it requires a massive collective response.

Allow me to take you through what I consider to be some of the key science – and I do this because I am thoroughly dismayed by the rise of the climate sceptics in the USA at the moment. I thought we had got past this point. Let me just remind you of what we are doing to our planet. The data is available, it is uncontroversial, it exists and it is very solid data from paleoclimatologists – in other words, people who study the past behaviour of our planetary system. The paleoclimatologists have accelerated their work massively over the last 20 years. When I used to talk about climate change, I spoke about the last 30,000 to 300,000 years, from the paleoclimatologists' work. Now we have data going back millions of years, so let me explain what I consider to be a really extraordinary outcome from the scientific effort. The paleoclimatologists can now go back in time to around 50 to 60 million years ago, when, we now know, the planet went through a temperature maximum. How high was the temperature then? Roughly 10 to 12°C higher on average than our pre-industrial level. At that temperature maximum, there was no ice left on the planet, in terms of ice sitting on large bodies, such as Greenland or Antarctica. Antarctica in fact at that point in time was a subtropical forest with large mammals, so underneath that ice, when you've gone three miles down you will find the memories of that period. It took 50 million years for Earth to cool down to the point where hominids began to appear.

Greenhouse gases were at a very high level, let's suggest about 1,500 parts per million, and it took a long time for the planet to recover from this very hot temperature.

Then the temperature became what I call *biphasic*, so the temperature was unstable. The planetary temperature was either cold or hot and didn't want to stay in either one of those two regions, but to sit between the two. The cold times were, of course, ice ages, and the other times, warm periods. At the present day, we are in a warm period. We have had lots of warm periods since this biostability began, caused by the motion of the planet around the Sun.

Now, if we look only at the last 400,000 years, there's a long ice age with very short warm periods roughly every hundred thousand years. This is our emergency, from the recent ice age to the present warm period. Eighteen thousand years ago, we began to emerge from the last ice age and we have been in the present warm period for twelve thousand years now, making it much the longest warm period on record. Begging the question, why is this one so much longer? Let me suggest the answer. As everyone knows, as the greenhouse gas levels go up, we have a warm period; and when they come down, we have an ice age.

For a warm period, the level is around 270 ppm and for an ice age around 200 ppm. There is a massive change in the planetary system between these two states, in the sense that during an ice age the sea level would be about 100 to 120 metres lower – so, during the last ice age, America and Russia were connected, which, you may suggest, would have been a good thing in modern history. As we emerge from an ice age, the ice on land melts into the oceans, the oceans warm up and both things drive the sea level up by 100 metres or so, so the map of the world changes as we go into and out of an ice age.

We have been amazingly fortunate to have this long ice age and therefore we have built 80 per cent of our cities right on the edge of our land masses, right where we can put boats into the oceans, Lisbon being a very good example.

I suggest that we have done that because we felt so secure with the map of the world as it was. As we emerge from that last ice age we see something unusual happening. The CO_2 level starts going up and this could well be the beginning of the world's first anthro-pocene, the first temperature period determined by humankind's behaviour. Why? Because we began to develop agriculture and in developing agriculture we started taking out forests, and forests removed CO_2 from the atmosphere, so we were removing part of the system that was keeping the CO_2 level in balance. And so this could be the reason why the CO_2 level began to go up. And it could be the reason why our warm period is lasting longer. That is just the beginning of the anthropocene.

The next step is the step that produced our well-being. If we look at our behaviour since the beginning of the industrial revo-lution, we see that fossil fuels have been fuelling the rise in our well-being. We have provided all of the energy for our develop-ment from fossil fuels.

Now, fossil fuels are naturally sequestered carbon, so the atmos-pheric CO_2 levels had been remarkably constant, between 200 and 270 ppm. Natural sequestration is part of that process. Then we discovered that we can burn fossil fuels to provide our energy and we have upset the balance, so that we are now at 389 ppm. We are going up at more than 2 ppm a year, and the rate of increase has been increasing.

How far back in time do we have to go before we get to roughly 389 ppm? About 3 million years. Good news! We've done enough to switch off the next ice age and I suggest that this *is* good news. However, we might have done that even before we began the industrial revolution; now we're overdoing it. The bad news is that if we carry on with this process we could certainly get back up to the early very high temperatures. If we burn all of the fossil fuels available then it could happen that temperatures could rise by 10 or 12°C. There's still lots of ice being melted, all that ice on Greenland. When that melts, the sea levels will go up six and a half metres. When the Antarctica ice melts, the sea level will go up another hundred metres.

We'd certainly get a big change in the map of the world then, with 80 per cent of our cities inundated at a much earlier stage than that. How long will that take? I don't know. There's no scientist who can tell you, if we go on like this, how long it will take to lose six metres worth of ice. Melting ice is a remarkably complicated process.

There is inertia in the climate system and this is because, to use a scientific term, of the heat capacity of the oceans – the oceans are warming up much more slowly than their ability to keep within the rate of increase in greenhouse gases. So there's roughly another 30 years of climate change ahead of us, anyway, even if we were to stop now at this number of 389 ppm. And that would then take us to a temperature rise roughly equivalent to the temperature 3 million years ago. Not a comfortable point, because even at 389 ppm, I cannot say as a scientist that we will stay below a 2°C temperature rise compared with the pre-industrial level. We already have a 0.7°C temperature rise compared with the pre-industrial level and to suggest we know how to stay below another 1.3°C is going beyond the science.

My colleagues and I at the new Smith School have calculated that since the beginning of the industrial revolution we have burnt about half a trillion tonnes of carbon from the natural sequestered coal, oil and gas that we have burnt. We also calculated that if we burn another half a trillion tonnes we will certainly go beyond this 2°C magic figure.

We have a massive dependence on fossil fuels and without good governance, good decisions from the international community, it is highly likely that we will go even beyond that one trillion tonne level.

So, what do we need to do? We are currently globally emitting around 36 billion tonnes of greenhouse gases, equivalent to 36 billion tonnes of carbon dioxide equivalent (CO_2^e). If we want to be on the stabilisation curve of 450 ppm – which itself does not guarantee a good future, but is the best, I think, we can hope for – if we want to be on that pathway, we need to reduce our emissions by a factor of two by mid-century. So, the 36 needs to come down to 18 billion tonnes of CO_2^e by mid-century. As I said, the global population will be 9 billion, so by simple arithmetic you can see that we each have to aim to be at or below two tonnes per person per annum of CO_2^e by mid-century.

When I was in the British Government, Britain had 11 tonnes per person per annum announced. Our objective was to reduce our emissions by 80 per cent by mid-century, which would take us down to 20 per cent of the current figure, which is 2.2 tonnes per person per annum. So the British Government figure is based on the hope that we will be on the stabilisation level indicated by the lower figure. What we are attempting to do – and Barroso has done a wonderful job in leading Europe on this campaign – is say this is not a matter of easing down to negotiate the best deal you can get at international negotiations; it is a matter of sitting down and saying this is what we're doing and almost shaming other countries into action.

I went to California to boast about the British Government's position on this. At this point I was saying we would make a 60 per cent reduction by 2050, and the Governor responded by saying if the Brits are saying 60 per cent reduction by 2050, we in California will reduce by 80 per cent by 2050. I thought that was a wonderful response, and that is the response we need if we are going to manage to be on track. So as we approach Copenhagen, this is what we need. If we are going for a global agreement this is the de minimis. What we need is to know where we are going; what is the global stabilisation level that we are aiming for? Is it 450 ppm, which is the figure I would like to see? We need a decision on the level we want to stabilise at, otherwise we don't know what the next steps in the process are. Once we have agreed that, we can set national targets. These are not national targets for ten years' time, but dynamic forward-looking targets reducing CO_2 emissions for each major nation and for each group of major nations as we move to mid-century, so that we arrive at that figure of two tonnes per person per annum. Once we have agreed on national targets then, based on these national dynamic forward-looking targets, we can introduce the next step, which is pricing CO_2. In Europe, the price is nearly high enough, although it has never been sufficiently high even when it was 28 euros a tonne. I would be looking for a figure in which carbon capture storage on a coal-fired power station made coal-fired power stations less economic than alternative energy sources, which would mean between 50 and 100 euros a tonne for CO_2. We need to price CO_2 to the point where the best and the cheapest way forward is to leave the carbon in the ground. That is, I'm afraid, the big challenge for the world.

Now, let me not forget Africa and the developing nations. We need to agree on convergence towards a global CO_2 cap-and-trade system. I'm an advisor to the President of Rwanda, President Kagame, and he made, I think, the most dramatic speech at Ban Ki-moon's UN meeting. He said: let us be part of the solution. Why don't we include African nations in the cap-and-trade process? Why don't we include all those nations that are below two tonnes per person per annum at the moment, so that we can trade CO_2 with nations that are above their projected future level.

That deals with several things at once. It deals with the problem that Gordon Brown and several others now draw attention to – that to manage this problem, developing nations need a massive transfer of funds – at least £100 billion. So instead of that being done by donations, why not include this in the trading process? As soon as you include African nations in the trading, you create a flow of money from the trading process. Let's not leave the developing nations out of this new global commodity, CO_2; not only because they will benefit from it, but also because if we do not include them, African nations will develop their economies by bringing in manufacturers from the West where CO_2 is heavily priced. They will bring these manufacturers in and build up their economies as high-carbon economies until we too have to pay a CO_2 price. This makes no sense at all. So let's move towards a global carbon-trading system.

I'd like now to make a few comments as a technologist. I do believe that it is science that has highlighted the problems of climate change and it's science and technology that need to provide the solutions.

Currently, the global energy demand can be represented by 175 ej per annum, where ej is the number of joules. This is not necessarily a good number. In fact, this 175 ej is a bad number in many places, so in Africa, much of the energy is provided by biomass but not with replaceable forests, rather through deforestation. What we want is to switch these sources into non-fossil-fuel-based sources as we move forward in time. Next, we can take electricity generation, conversion devices, passive systems and then we end up with final services. We need to be looking at energy efficiency gains and we need to look at defossilisation. What I suggest, and suggest to the private-sector companies I work with in Oxford, is that this is a massive opportunity for those who believe in world creation through dynamic inventions, taking hold of existing technologies and bringing them to the marketplace.

So there are a number of possible ways forward. Let me just give you one rather startling fact: 470–475 ej is the global world energy source demand at the moment. If I measure this in terms of final services, only 55 ej is converted to final services. The difference between 470–475 and 55 ej shows that there is a massive energy loss in all of those processes, so the big financial gain and the big gain for climate change is in efficiency. In the conversion processes that we are talking about, there's an enormous amount of headroom. Yes, we do necessarily lose poor-quality heat, but we can minimise those losses and we can even maximise our usage of that heat.

I just want to remind you about the oil costs to the global economy. I hope the Gulbenkian Foundation will forgive me for making these comments. The total oil costs to the economy can be expressed in terms of the passage of money from the rest of the world to the Middle East. Annually 1.7 trillion dollars is the best estimate.

Anyone who says to me as an economist that they can calculate what the cost of managing to defossilise our economies will be, I question seriously. I do not believe we can calculate that impact; it depends on how effectively we manage our own economies without importing oil – for example, instead of sending that money into the Middle East as a kind of a global tax, we would be spending the money in our own countries. We will see, I believe, if we do this properly, a massive spur to our economies. I have a further comment, if I may wander a little from the point; what to date has been the cost of the Iraq War? Why do I mention the Iraq War? Because I believe the Iraq War will in future times be seen by historians as the first of the great twenty-first-century resource wars.

The Iraq War has an awful lot to do with the fact that the USA had already passed its peak oil production and needed to look around to secure friendly governments in places with large oil supplies. The cost of that war was 3 trillion dollars. The outcome of that war was certainly no guarantee of security.

I went to the White House in 2001, sent by my Prime Minister, a tough man, to persuade the White House that the decision to abandon Kyoto was not a good one. I got a very straight answer back from the White House: America cannot afford to price CO_2, America cannot afford to go down that route. Let me tell you, if America had spent one-tenth of those 3 trillion dollars on the Iraq War on defossilising its energy sources, it would have become independent of oil imports, and it would have made a massive investment in its own economic future.

I'm an optimist, and let me say why I'm an optimist, why I think this can be managed. Let me use a saying, 'Necessity is the mother of invention.' We have not had to look for alternative energy sources before. Of course we know how to manage this problem. How much of the solar energy reaching the Earth's surface do we need to convert to usable energy for 9 billion people to live well on this planet? The answer is, a rather small proportion of that which reaches the Earth's surface. In other words, we have an abundant source of energy: we have direct solar heating, already a technology that is out there. I'm afraid my chemical physics colleagues are a bit lazy. They know about silicon because of the enormous effort going into microchips, so, when asked to produce solar photovoltaics, what do they do? They use silicon, which is inherently expensive. We must use solar photovoltaics that are made of ceramics, that are made of plastics, that are made of paint, so that architects can use these materials on the outside of every building and can still design beautiful buildings such as the one we're in now. There is no earthly reason why the effort put into these areas should not produce good results.

I suggest, and this follows directly from the earlier comments, that what we need is a paradigm shift. If we are going to face up to these problems, we need a system for collective response. I am suggesting that our global governance procedures need to be re-examined. We had a very forward-looking President of the United States at the end of the Second World War who said, we don't want to continue to repeat these world wars, and what emerged was the United Nations. I am going to suggest that the structure of the UN is no longer fit for purpose in the twenty-first century. The great powers that sat on the Security Council and still sit on the Security Council are no longer relevant to a problem where we need global representation on that body to get to the nub of the problem and develop agreement. I do think that as we move forward in time we are in a relatively good place, because we have a visionary President in the White House. I would also suggest we have visionary leadership in China. I think both President Jintao and Premier Jiabao have a remarkably far-sighted view of the importance of ecosystem services; they do understand them. If we could just get these two sets of leaders together I believe the rest of the world would pull in behind them.

Sustainable consumption becomes the key. The consumption process that produced the wealth of our nations in the twentieth century is not relevant to the twenty-first, for all the reasons I'm giving you. Consumption has two meanings, of course: we consume to improve ourselves and our well-being, but also to improve our status, and this becomes competitive. I drive a bigger car than you, so I have a higher status. But this is consuming the resources of the planet; we are using up the resources of the planet at a rate far faster than they are being replenished. For example, we are mismanaging our resources of fresh water, and in particular I would want to draw attention to the oceans and the atmosphere.

We have not always mismanaged and I will finish on what I hope is a slightly upbeat note. Let's look at this paradigm shift I'm talking about: there are many things to block that shift. We need an enormous appetite from around the world for this shift and we should not have to wait for another disaster to envelop us before we act. In fact, we cannot afford it. We need a twenty-first-century renaissance. I suggest that term 'renaissance' because it has got a positive sense. We need a culture that comes back to thinking about our natural resources, our ecosystem services first and foremost; we need economics that address the problem of sustainability and perhaps we need to see the death of one number percentage increase in GDP, as the number by which we judge how well governments are doing. That number has no further relevance in the twenty-first century because it does not account for what we are doing to our planet's resources.

The challenges to the paradigm shift I am suggesting are national priorities, which always seem to take priority over global priorities. We will not resolve this set of problems. So, national perceptions versus global priorities. This alternative future for us on the planet becomes one in which we try to tackle problems together, and we have to. We need to move away from what the Chicago School of economists has so triumphantly developed as the sole economic model for development.

There is a bit of a silver lining to the current financial crisis. We know that exponential growth does not continue necessarily into the future. The other piece of silver lining, and I hesitate to say this because I am not suggesting we need economic crises to manage this, is that in 2008, CO_2 emissions were roughly four and a half per cent below the business as usual expectation and this year will be even further below that, and by 2020, global emissions will be around 15 to 25 per cent below business as usual, as a result of the current economic crisis. There's a little window of opportunity there because we have got a slightly longer time scale to manage the problem. As for nostalgic romanticism, I hope I can dismiss quickly the idea that we had it all right in the eighteenth century, so let us forego all the science and technology that we can have.

I do want to address some comments critically to the science community. There is a massive opportunity for science and engineering technology to attack the problems I am talking about, but there's a cost in setting up alternative attractive features for the scientific community. This is not only a financial cost, but a cost in brain power too. I fear that we have developed into a society in which we know more about landing a vehicle in Mars than we know about developing low-carbon energy sources, than we know about managing malaria, HIV/AIDS, and so on. Our focuses in the scientific community have to change as we go through the paradigm shift.

We can take, as an example, what our society has done to the Earth's atmosphere. Consider cars: the combustion engine driven on petrol produces awful fumes, carbon monoxide, gases and so on. Through our behaviour and technology we are at the point where, if we were to bring even a diesel engine car meeting Europe's five standards into this room at this point in time and run the engine, it would clean up the air in this room. Enormous advances have gone into the manufacture of cars to produce more efficient traps and catalytic systems. We have learned how to tackle these problems and I suggest that we need to take advice from the scientific community and handle the problems that are on our doorstep now.

In my work at the University of Oxford, we work with the private sector, with academics and with governments to find solutions. So far we have established a Low Carbon Mobility Centre and a Private Sector Transformation Centre, which are working with the private sector to defossilise the economy. I am working with the high-carbon sectors in particular. We want to work where we can get the biggest impact on climate and development, particularly in the developing world.

As we move forward, we need to see that we are able to look to the mid-century as something that is nearly upon us, and we need to look forward with some optimism. I'd like to quote from Pindar, the Greek poet, whose philosophy can, I think, be expressed by this simple statement: 'Oh, my soul seek not after immortal life but exhaust the limits of the possible.'

We have it within our capability; it is possible to manage these many problems, but it does require us to act collectively and to gear our culture to make this renaissance.

Has Biodiversity a Future?

MIGUEL BASTOS ARAÚJO

The future of biodiversity is a far from trivial challenge for at least two reasons. First, the key to understanding the future of biodiversity is partly tied up with understanding the past. Unfortunately, we only have fragmented pieces of evidence to reconstruct the patterns and processes associated with the diversification of life on Earth. These pieces are not random. They are biased, since not all taxa are equally well preserved through the fossil record, and not all regions preserve fossils equally well. Secondly, even if we had a representative and unbiased knowledge of the past, we know, from the words of Mark Twain, that 'history doesn't repeat itself but it rhymes' or, to use the famous quote by Yogi Berra, 'the future ain't what it used to be'. In other words, understanding the past does not provide clues for making predictions about the future. It does help, however, in thinking critically about temporal processes and this is what I shall attempt here. I shall begin by briefly describing what we presently know about biodiversity and extinctions in *deep time*. In particular, I will refer to the five big mass extinction events. These events have been inferred from analysis of the fossil record. Then, I shall discuss evidence for extinction events occurring in *shallow time*. That is, the recent period starting in the end of the Tertiary, roughly 1.8 million years ago. Finally, I discuss contemporary extinctions in the context of past extinctions and ask whether we are witnessing a sixth mass extinction.

Planet Earth originated 4.5 billion years ago (abbreviated 4.5 ga BP, for gigayears before present). In the beginning there were bacteria (3.5 ga BP). The long interval between 3.5 and 0.6 ga BP is known as the Precambrian. The fossil record is sparse for this period, but first evidence of photosynthesis is recorded about 2 ga BP, and the first eukaryotes are reported for 1.9 ga BP. An extraordinary number of life forms are thought to have originated during the so-called Cambrian explosion at 0.57 ga BP. This is when our story starts.

I will focus mainly on extinctions because this is what is more relevant for understanding the near future. Global extinctions can happen in matters of days, while speciation – the formation of new species – is a longer process that typically takes more than a couple of million years. Most extinction events (c. 95 per cent of all extinctions) occur in the background. The background includes relatively non-dramatic periods that mediate the pulses above background, which are termed mass extinctions. Extinctions in the background are not caused by major catastrophes. They are caused by small changes in climate, depleted resources, competition, disease and other changes that require adaptation and flexibility. In turn, mass extinctions are extraordinary events. They usually are extinctions that (1) occur all over the world (they are not regional events); (2) involve large numbers of species (proportions often greater than half of the world's biodiversity); (3) involve many types of species (not particular branches of the tree of life); and (4) occur over a short geological time (unlike background extinctions).

It is generally accepted that there have been five great mass extinctions during the history of life: one each in the end-Ordovician, late-Devonian, end-Permian, end-Triassic and end-Cretaceous (also known as K-T, standing for the boundary between the Cretaceous[1] and the Tertiary periods). The most famous is probably the K-T extinction as it represented the end of the dinosaurs, but virtually all plant and animal groups lost species and genera in this period. Marine animals saw the disappearance of 34 per cent of their genera and among land animals the hit was higher.

What might have triggered such high numbers of species loss? Background extinctions are often caused by biological factors, the most important of which are problems associated with small population sizes (e.g. demographic stochasticity, genetic and social deterioration). Competition may also play an important role, especially when faunas and floras that evolved in isolation are brought together by natural processes of invasion, or by external geological events, such as the merging of previously isolated land masses.[2] But typically, such biological factors have local to regional impacts and do not affect all of biodiversity indiscriminately. So, physical causes need to be invoked to explain mass extinctions.

The most popular of which is what David M. Raup termed, 'rocks falling out of the sky'. There is now evidence inviting the interpretation that the K-T extinction was caused by a large meteorite falling down in the Yucatan peninsula. This extraterrestrial event is thought to have caused a range of direct (e.g. a large tsunami) and indirect events (e.g. the shutdown of photosynthesis caused by the debris cloud) that might have triggered extinctions. One of the most intriguing hypotheses about mass extinctions is called the nemesis hypothesis. This hypothesis proposes that there is a periodicity of c. 26 million years to mass extinctions, which arises because of collision with meteorites from the Oort Cloud[3] as they are perturbed in their orbits by a dark star (a companion of the sun). There is much debate over the periodicity of mass extinctions and evidence for the existence of the Oort Cloud is still missing.

Other physical mechanisms have been proposed to explain mass extinctions of the past. They often involve environmental changes of great magnitude. For example, climate change due to intense volcanic activity or continental drift has been proposed. In both cases changes can occur abruptly. Continental drift may cause splitting or merging of land masses, causing changes in ocean currents and thus prompting abrupt alterations in the distribution of heat across the globe. Changes in sea level also rank high among the alternative hypotheses, particularly for aquatic environments. Finally, environmental changes involving depletion of oxygen in shallow marine environments, changes in the salinity of ocean water, acid rain, dust and aerosols are all candidate culprits for mass extinctions.

Research into the causes of mass extinctions will continue. Two facts are known: (1) mass extinctions wiped out great numbers of species from all groups worldwide, but they also contributed to shaping the evolution of life (their consequences continued to be felt and have an impact for around 5 million years following each episode); (2) mass extinctions are rare episodes, triggered by extraordinary environmental or extraterrestrial events.

If there have been only five mass extinctions and if they were likely caused by extraordinary events, were cyclical climate changes in the past not causing major extinctions? To address this question, I propose to take a close look at evidence of extinctions occurring in shallow time, that is, in the past 1.8 million years – a period best known as the Pleistocene.

The Pleistocene was characterised by sequences of glacial and interglacial periods. Glacial periodicity shifted about 900,000 years ago from cycles of c. 41,000 years to cycles of c. 100,000 years. These glaciations, which are thought to have numbered more than 20, varied in severity, but had profound effects on the distributions of fauna and flora. For example, changes in temperature during the Pleistocene led to continual changes in sea level, which in turn altered the sizes and configurations of land masses. During cold periods, water was trapped inland in the form of ice, and the sea level dropped, causing enlargement and merging of previously disconnected land masses (e.g. Britain was connected with France). In contrast, during warmer periods the sea level rose, thus causing a reduction of land masses and increasing their fragmentation. Given the massive climatic and bio-geographical changes occurring during the Pleistocene, did species go extinct in great numbers?

Not quite. There is evidence that 68 per cent of tree genera went extinct from Europe during the Pliocene–Pleistocene transition, but only one tree species is known to have been lost from North America during the same period. Massive extinctions were reported among the megafauna, that is, species of more than 44 kg. A review by Koch and Barnosky[4] suggests that unlike in trees, extinctions among the megafauna were global: 88% extinct genera in Australia, 83% in South America, 72% in North America, 35% in Eurasia, 21% in Africa. These extinctions had two features in common. The first is that they affected large-bodied animals. The second is that they occurred in the period of time starting 40,000 years ago until recently.

There is much debate regarding the causes of Pleistocene megafauna extinctions. Even though there are mysteries to uncover, such as the megafauna extinctions in South America, there is a general consensus that the expansion of human populations, or some combination of human influence and climate change, are part of the explanation. For example, the woolly mammoth in Eurasia is now thought to have become extinct as a consequence of two processes. The first would have been temperature increases that pushed populations northwards and caused reduction and fragmentation of grassland habitats. This process would have caused a general decline of the Eurasian populations. The second process would have been interaction with humans (possibly as a consequence of hunting). Humans are thought to have given the *coup de grâce* to the small populations of mammoths surviving in northern glacial refugia.[5]

Extinctions between the Pleistocene till now can be grouped into three phases. Phase 1 corresponds to the Pliocene–Pleistocene transition. This is when the generally warmer and wetter climates of the Pliocene gave rise to cooler and dryer climates of the Pleistocene. Major shifts in the distributions of biomes are known for this period. For example, the laurel forests dominating most of southern Europe were gradually substituted by sclerophyll forests and shrubs. As mentioned above, extinctions are recorded for trees in Europe but not in North America, a phenomenon recently termed as the Quaternary Conundrum by Botkin et al.[6] Phase 2 corresponds to the Pleistocene–Holocene transition, when most terrestrial megafauna went extinct. This is the period starting in the last glaciation until now. Because climate oscillations were common during the Pleistocene, without any evidence for selective kill of large mammals being presented, and because megafauna extinctions coincided roughly with the last migration of anatomically modern humans out of Africa, the current view is that humans were the ultimate drivers of megafauna extinction. Note that human impacts were likely analogous to the impacts of 'invasive species' when they encounter native fauna and flora that are not adapted to the competitively superior abilities of the invader. Phase 2 can thus be generalised so to include all human-induced invasions causing major extinctions of local fauna and flora. Such a mechanism of extinction includes the continent-wide extinctions of megafauna caused by the out-of-Africa migration of anatomically modern humans, but also the more recent extinctions caused by European navigators colonising and introducing animals and plants to Oceanic islands on their way to India and America (a famous example being the goats introduced by the Portuguese to the island of Santa Helena that have caused the extinction of its rich endemic flora). Phase 3 corresponds to the large-scale modifications of habitats and ecosystems that have taken place since the invention of agriculture until now. Currently, 24 per cent of the net primary productivity of the planet is appropriated by humans and our activities occupy more than 35 per cent of the land surface. Extinctions in Phase 3 are, therefore, extinctions caused by competition for resources.

None of the above phases caused a mass sixth extinction in the sense defined above. However, some authors suggest we may now be on the verge of a sixth mass extinction. What evidence is there for such a statement?

Measuring extinctions in real time is difficult. Not least because our calculus of biodiversity is very incomplete. So far, 1.8 million species have been described, but estimates invite the interpretation that 5 to 40 million species exist on Earth. Of these 1.8 million species, only 44,838 (2.5%) have been assessed for their threat status (values from the 2008 International Union for Conservation of Nature assessment). Of the assessed species, 869 (1.9%) are reported as extinct, while 257 (0.6%) are possibly extinct; 38% of the assessed species are considered threatened with extinction, 8% are near threatened and 12% have insufficient data. Are these estimates representative of the world's biodiversity? Probably not, since the assessed species are far from being a random sample of the total pool of existing species.

To overcome the lack of representativeness of the IUCN assessments researchers have sought to provide estimates of extinction risk based on species-area curves[7] or extrapolations from IUCN red list assessments. These estimates are then compared to background extinction estimates from the fossil record to assert whether current extinctions are in tune with background levels. So, for example, if one assumes that there are 10 million species on Earth (a conservative estimate) and that background extinctions from the fossil record are 1 species being lost per million species per year, then the estimated total number of species becoming extinct in the background should be 10 per year. Using species-area curves, Edward Wilson calculates that 27,000 species are currently lost each year. It is estimated that 22 per cent of all species might be expected to have become extinct by 2020, if no action is taken to prevent this. Using a different methodology, based on extrapolations from the current IUCN red lists, Georgina Mace provides an estimate of 14 to 22 per cent of species and sub-species being lost over the next hundred years. The two analyses yield very different results, but both concur with current extinctions being well above background rates.

The above estimates are not without problems. Species-area curves were proposed to predict how many species should be found on islands of different sizes, but their use in predictions of extinctions risk is far from consensual. Extrapolations from IUCN red list assessments are also problematic, because the assessed species are taxonomically and regionally biased and there is no evidence that extinctions should be equivalent for the non-assessed species. Finally, background extinctions are averaged across very long time periods (deep time) and they hide oscillations that may be very large and well above the long-term trend. So, comparing short-time extinctions with long-term background rates may not provide statistically significant information for comparing current extinctions with the background rate.

With the available information we can say with confidence that extinctions and threats to species persistence are occurring globally and over a short geological time. However, for contemporary extinctions to qualify as a mass extinction there would be a need for very large numbers and many different types of species to become extinct. There is no evidence for either one of the two last criteria, but that does not necessarily mean that they are not taking place. It is rather the case that the information is not there, or that the tipping points have not yet been reached.

Furthermore, the three extinction phases described above do not provide a comprehensive picture of the contemporary pressures on biodiversity. Arguably, the impacts associated with Phase 3 (habitat modification) are still under way globally. Human population growth and increases in the per capita appropriation of resources by humans are bound to increase, thus reducing the amount of energy and space left for other species. The impacts of biological invasions described in Phase 2 are still occurring. As trade becomes truly global, more invasive species are spread across the world and new impacts on native biodiversity are triggered. Finally, contemporary climate changes are already causing species to change their phenology and distributions, with greater impacts being projected for the twenty-first century.

The impact of contemporary climate change is expected to be more dramatic in the colder edges of the world, with entire communities of arctic and alpine species projected to disappear as temperatures increase and they find nowhere else to go. The warmer and drier places are also likely to face dramatic changes, as increases in aridity may force species to subsist beyond their tolerance levels. In other regions, climate change would force species to shift away from their present locations. In the past, species have been able to adapt by tracking a suitable climate by dispersing, and some species are reported to have been moving northwards in response to recent warming. For example, in the United Kingdom a study showed that a large number of animal species from various taxonomic groups shifted their distributions northwards over a recent 30-year period.[8] The question is whether many species will have such an option. In other words, whether several of the species surviving in protected areas have the ability to (1) find suitable habitats elsewhere; and (2) reach suitable habitats elsewhere by dispersing through often hostile landscapes.

I argue that adding climate change on the top of the familiar threats to biodiversity causes additional challenges that may prove insurmountable. It seems species are now being exposed to a combination of all the threats noted above: climate change is projected to intensify in the twenty-first century and occur over a very short period of time (as for extinctions in Phase 1); biological invasions are expanding due to the workings of a truly global economy (as for extinctions in Phase 2); and habitat modification is being intensified in several parts of the world due to human population growth (as for Phase 3). The combination of these three sources of threat and their synergies is likely to cause a new extinction phase (Phase 4), which could potentially lead to a sixth mass extinction unless proactive conservation strategies are put in place.

I began with the question, 'Has biodiversity a future?' The answer is clearly, yes. Biodiversity has survived grim days before, and there is no reason to expect this time will be different. But we are indeed putting a strain on the world's biodiversity as we know it today. We share this planet with a biodiversity that co-evolved with us, and that allowed us to strive and become a dominant species. If we were to cause a sixth mass extinction, biodiversity would eventually recover as it has done in the past. It would not be a quick process (in the past, it took c. 5 million years for biodiversity to recover from mass extinctions). We do not even know what life forms would emerge from a current extinction crisis and whether they would allow for any form of civilisation. But one thing we know: a mass extinction in our times would cause the human species to live in a biodiversity-impoverished world for the rest of our existence. I personally do not like the prospect, and I believe most of us do not approve of it either.

Notes

1 K is used instead of C to avoid confusion with the Carboniferous and Cambrian periods.

2 The Great American Biotic Interchange is one of the more famous of such events.
3 The Oort Cloud (also called Nemesis) is a cloud of rocks and dust that is thought to surround our solar system. In the course of a 26-million-year orbit, the cloud would sweep close enough to our part of the solar system to bring comet showers down to Earth. The Oort Cloud was named after Jan H. Oort who proposed its existence in 1950.
4 P.L. Koch and A.D. Barnosky, 'Late Quaternary Extinctions: State of the Debate', *Annual Review of Ecology, Evolution and Systematics* 37, 2006, pp. 215–50.
5 D. Nogués-Bravo et al., 'Climate Change, Humans and the Extinction of the Woolly Mammoth', *PLoS Biology* 6, 2008, e79. doi: 10.1371/journal.pbio.0060079.
6 D. Botkin et al., 'Forecasting Effects of Global Warming on Biodiversity', *BioScience* 57, 2007, pp. 227–36.
7 A species-area curve describes the relationship between the area of a given region and the number of species found within that region. The larger the area, the larger the numbers of species expected to be found in it. The relationship between area and species numbers follows a mathematical power function. Let S be the number of species, A be the area and c and z be the constants, then the power function species-area relationship should be: $S = cA^z$. Applications of species-area curves to predict extinctions typically start with predictions of habitat (e.g. forest) loss (the A in the equation) to then estimate the resulting S.
8 R. Hickling et al., 'The Distributions of a Wide Range of Taxonomic Groups are Expanding Polewards', *Global Change Biology* 12, 2006, pp. 450–55.

The Ethical Challenge of Sustainability in Water Management

PEDRO ARROJO AGUDO

Introduction and Overview

The 1,100 million people who have no guaranteed access to potable water are the human face of the crisis of unsustainability that we have caused in continental aquatic ecosystems. This crisis is not actually a problem of shortage of resources: in places where once one could drink potable water, now the most vulnerable communities (the poor) are getting sick and poisoned, particularly in the case of children.

The second aspect of this crisis of unsustainability is the destruction and degradation of fishery resources, a clear indication of the crisis of biodiversity in continental aquatic areas. This has aggravated problems of hunger as fishing provides the 'poor man's protein'. The degradation of rivers, lakes, salt marshes and mangroves affects not only freshwater fishing, or transition water fishing, but also marine coastal fishing, which is fertilised by the massive supplies of continental nutrients.

Large dams, besides having a serious social impact on displaced populations (about 80 million people), have also had a negative influence on fluvial habitats, leading to the extinction of numerous species of fish and shellfish. On the other hand, drastic changes in flood cycles have had a major impact on the floodplains and traditional ways of farming and cattle breeding, which millions depend upon for food.

The crisis of unsustainability of aquatic ecosystems and aquifers has severely reduced the resilience of the continental water cycle, which implies an increasing risk of droughts, storms and other extreme climatic events that will worsen with the climatic change in progress. On the other hand, there is an increase in the deterioration of deltas (subsidence) and coastal ecosystems (through the destruction of mangroves, the collapse of solids, fluxes and sands retained in large dams, etc.) in a convergent synergy with the rises in sea levels due to global warming.

The social impact of this lack of sustainability in aquatic ecosystems is accentuated when it converges with two other thorny issues: inequality and poverty, on the one hand, and governance in relation to the management of basic water resources and sanitation services, on the other. This worsens with the pressures of privatisation inherent in the current globalisation model.

Due to this global crisis in water management, a new ethical approach is needed to distinguish different water categories: lifewater, associated with human rights; citizenship-water, for general use and associated with citizenship rights; and economy-water, for productive uses but not related to levels for a decent life. This water differentiation must take into account the relevant use priority and involve specific management criteria for the different ethical water categories. I shall now address these issues in more detail.

The Global Water Crisis

The systematic and widespread degradation of the continental aquatic ecosystems has supposedly destroyed the fluvial and marine fishing activities that are essential to a proteinic diet for millions of people. It has also destroyed the traditional ways of farming and cattle breeding associated with the fluvial cycles. However, perhaps the most dramatic impact has been on the 1,100 million people without access to potable water because of the degradation and contamination of their traditional water sources.

In this critical context, the current globalisation model, which largely ignores the most basic ethical principles, is aggravating the situation. Instead of reducing ecological degradation, it is accelerating the depletion of resources and the collapse of the continental hydrological cycle. In addition to this, it has not reduced wealth inequality nor guaranteed the poorest sections of society their most basic rights, especially their human rights, such as access to potable water or decent sanitation. Environmental values and basic services of general interest to citizens are today part of the commercial trade that obeys only economic values.

The origins of this global water crisis are rooted in three major failures:

- the crisis of **unsustainability**, of rivers, lakes, wetlands, aquifers and related ecosystems (forests, coastal ecosystems, etc.);

- the crisis of **poverty and inequity**, with the correlated problems of vulnerability;

- the crisis of the **governance** of basic services, such as those of water supply and sanitation.

The Crisis of Unsustainability and Poverty as Key Issues in Access to Potable Water

In all ancient cultures we can find the paradigm of 'mother nature'. From a mythical point of view, this paradigm shows nature as a mother, a generator and a supporter of life. The Renaissance spirit changed this approach by adding a new paradigm: that of the 'dominance of nature'. The father of scientific empiricism, Francis Bacon, said in a ruthless affirmation that science should torture nature, as the Holy Office of the Inquisition tortured its prisoners, to discover its ultimate secrets.

A Spanish scientist from the early twentieth century began his inaugural speech at the Real Academia de las Ciencias by quoting precisely the paradigm of mother nature. The speech exalts nature's beauty such as to 'generate our passion and love', developing into a new mythification, again putting nature in parallel with the feminine gender, but this time from the point of view of a lover that is the object of man's desire. His speech used the same idea as a way of highlighting the irrational, unstable, changeable and unpredictable character of nature, characteristics also attributed to the female sex; this motivated the rational and firm actions of science, governed by clear masculine profiles, to dominate nature and to make it serve man. This is essentially the Romantic approach, which is undoubtedly friendlier than Bacon's, and the one that has supported the paradigm of the domination of nature until the present day.[1]

Supported by this logic, and with a blind faith in techno-scientific development, significant improvements have certainly been achieved in the quality of life of billions of people. However, at the same time, nature's natural balance has been affected, which has meant heavy costs, especially for the poorest sections of society and future generations. The most significant of all, without a doubt, is the multifaceted problem of access to potable water for millions of people.

With reference to water resources, the systematic destruction and degradation of water ecosystems and aquifers has already led to dramatic social repercussions: 1,100 million people with no guaranteed access to drinking water and the breakdown of the hydrologic cycle and health of rivers, lakes and wetlands are two consequences of this crisis.

This is how the *European Declaration for a New Water Culture*, signed in 2005 by a hundred scientists from the different countries of the European Union, began.

1,100 million people without guaranteed access to potable water; over 2,500 million without basic sanitation services; or a forecast of 1,600,000 annual deaths due to diarrhoea caused by poor quality water (a figure that does not include sickness caused by drinking water contaminated with heavy metals and other toxic products, which cause medium or long-term deaths)... Inevitably these are facts that define the situation as a Global Water Crisis.[2]

Given these facts, we often face predictions based on an alleged shortage of water resources, together with a growing world population. Sometimes there are even predictions of the desiccation of the planet due to climatic change.

The reality is that the Blue Planet we live on, the Water Planet, will remain blue unless an asteroid collides with the Earth and radically changes the current natural balance. Global warming will generate higher levels of evaporation and greater precipitation (what goes up, goes down), accelerating and unbalancing the hydrological cycle. It is certain that the difficulty 1,100 million people have in accessing potable water is not so much due to a lack of water, but rather the quality of what is available. All communities have settled near a river, a spring, a lake, or in places where groundwater can be reached through wells. Usually, the problem is that previously potable water is now contaminated. By degrading the health of aquatic ecosystems, first you kill the frogs and fish and then people get sick and die, especially the most vulnerable – the children from the poorest communities.

Undoubtedly, among these 1,100 million people, a significant minority have problems of physical access to water. We are referring to people living in semi-arid areas, traditionally at the edge of habitable zones, such as the African Sahel, which now may become virtually impossible to live in if climate change continues apace. However, many of those 1,100 million people live in humid wetlands, where the current model of development, the lack of information and education, the irresponsibility of states and the immoral greed of companies, have led to an unparalleled crisis of unsustainability in rivers, lakes, wetlands and aquifers.

What these hundreds of millions of people in both semi-arid and humid areas have in common is poverty, and often, extreme poverty. We face a humanitarian crisis, which threatens to affect 4,000 million people by 2025 if we allow these trends to take their course.

The voices often heard in international forums and institutions justify the difficulties in solving these problems by the scale of the financial effort required. Such arguments are unacceptable at this point. We are not facing a financial challenge, but rather a political challenge, in the noble, Aristotelian sense of 'political': a challenge of priority, in terms of what we understand as *res publica*, 'matter for all'. The lack of political will, both nationally and internationally, is blatant and shameful, even when it comes to achieving the Millennium Development Goals established by the UN. One of these goals specifically mentions 'reducing, by half, the percentage of people without access to potable water or basic sanitation by 2015'. This would mean 274,000 people getting access to potable water and basic sanitation for the first time every day until 2015. Achieving this goal would cost less than 3,000 million euros per year for 10 years, which is the monthly expenditure on mineral water bottles in Europe and the USA; or a fraction of the over 500,000 million euros of public funds intended to support the financial giants that, paradoxically, are the main culprits behind the economic disaster in which we find ourselves.

There are several causes of this ecological crisis: massive reductions in flows, drastic changes in natural regimes and the disruption of the continuity of fluvial habitats, all due to the construction of large dams, which have also caused the alteration of solid flows and the reduction of sediment in reservoirs; drainage and desiccation of wetlands, which has affected their regulating and depuration functions; massive deforestation, with corresponding erosion and its impacts on the water cycle (more surface run-off and less water infiltration to aquifers); channelling and drainage occupying large areas in zones normally affected by natural river floods, with their consequent effects on biodiversity, nutrient flows and increased risk of flooding in the low-lying areas of river basins. Certainly, one of the main causes of this ecological collapse is the systematic and massive contamination of rivers, lakes and aquifers. It is an organic and biological contamination caused by discharges from urban, agricultural and cattle-rearing activities, and the toxic character of industrial, mining and even agricultural activities.

The discharge of sewage into the natural environment and the infiltration of septic tank effluents into aquifers cause serious water contamination. Diarrhoea from drinking such waters is now one of the main causes of infant mortality, with over 4,000 children under five years old dying every day.

On the other hand, diffuse pollution from agriculture is becoming increasingly serious. The massive and widespread use of chemical fertilisers and pesticides is making agriculture the primary source of contamination in many areas. Diffuse contamination is extremely difficult to control, and together with urban sewage, produces eutrophication processes that lead to the destruction of life in the water environment through the excess of nutrients present.

In the industry and mining sectors, the lack of international regulatory measures and national laws, or corruption and laxness in applying them, mean that discharges and the use of obsolete production techniques are permitted, which contaminate and are a danger to public health in the majority of poor and developing countries. These techniques are more 'profitable' for companies, which are often multinationals boasting an image of social responsibility and respect for the environment in the developed countries from whence they come.

The proliferation of open-pit mining is particularly serious because it pollutes fluvial headwater areas with mining leachates and heavy metals, cyanide discharges and other toxins. In the region of Cajamarca (Peru), for example, indigenous communities suffer serious illnesses caused by gold mining. In the Pilcomayo (Bolivia), fishing has disappeared and horticulture languishes because irrigation water has, it is believed, been contaminated by Potosi mining activities. The aggressive expansion of these kinds of businesses has led to cases such as that of Pascua Lama, where one of the mining multinationals, the Canadian Barrick, has successfully obtained concessions from the Chilean and Argentine governments to exploit a gold mine under a glacier. In this case, not even the social alarm generated by climate change and the importance of glaciers as regulators of the river sources seems to offer sufficient grounds to stop the greed of the richest. In Argentina's Mendoza province, however, a citizen's movement upholds legislation prohibiting open-pit mining, in order to protect not only public health but also the economy of the region, which is based on international recognition and appreciation of their wines.

The Crisis of Unsustainability and Poverty: Impacts on the Food Crisis

There are devastating direct and indirect impacts on the sources of food production in the world, created by the unsustainability crisis in rivers, lakes and wetlands.

Fishing is, in fact, the main source of protein in many impoverished communities and countries. In Africa, fishing represents more than 20 per cent of animal protein, and in Asia 30 per cent.[3] It is no wonder that fish is said to be the poor man's protein.

Throughout the twentieth century, the construction of large dams has destroyed river fishing by causing many species to become extinct. This has occurred in Urrá (Colombia), Singkarak (Sumatra), Lingjintan (China), Theun Hiboun (Laos) and Pak Mun (Thailand), among others. In these cases, the food problems created have affected and continue to affect hundreds of thousands of poor families in riparian communities.[4]

Particularly enlightening is the case of Lake Tonle Sap or Big Lake in Cambodia, in the hydrographic basin of the Mekong.[5] The lake is not only a key factor in regulation, but also works as a veritable 'breathing apparatus'. With a surface area that varies between 3,000 km^2 and 13,000 km^2 (when it receives the massive monsoon flows), the lake generates one of the world's most fertile fishing grounds, with 400 species of fish and 100,000 tonnes of fish caught annually, representing the main proteinic source of 9.5 million Cambodians. The periodic flooding of those 10,000 km^2 of fields and forests provides the appropriate habitat for fish to spawn, taking advantage of the wealth of nutrients generated there.

On the other hand, before coming to the delta, the periodic flooding of the Mekong and its tributaries fertilises floodplains in a natural cycle that allows the growth of about 50 per cent of the rice produced in Cambodia. An estimated 52 million people depend on the river for their basic diet. Nowadays, Thailand's accelerated industrial growth is encouraging the construction of large dams and river-channelling systems that threaten to create an ecological breakdown in the basin and particularly in the delta.

In the Amazon, home to over 3,000 species of fish, 200,000 tonnes of fish are caught annually, mostly for domestic consumption and local markets. However, the emergence of industrial fishing, deforestation, mining discharges, dam construction and wetland drainage is causing species such as the emblematic tambaqui to become extinct.

Over the last decade, real ecological disasters have been produced in large lagoon systems and these have resulted in several humanitarian disasters due to the devastation of fishing resources. In Lake Chad, the weakening of the monsoon and long droughts due to current climate change led to the surface area being reduced by 80 per cent, transforming Africa's fourth-biggest lake into a wetland that can be traversed on foot.

In the Aral Sea, 90 per cent of the flows of the Amu Darya and Syr Darya rivers was deviated to irrigate plantations of export cotton. The area was reduced from 64,500 km^2 to 30,000 km^2, increasing salinity by a factor of three, wiping out 44,000 tonnes of annual fishing and 60,000 jobs.[6]

In Lake Victoria, the introduction of exotic species (such as Nile perch) for industrial fishing for export has created a humanitarian catastrophe by destroying traditional fishing, which was the main source of sustenance for riverbank communities.

In Bangladesh, in just two decades, the fishing industry and international marketing have increased the volume of catches. This has caused problems of overfishing, which, paradoxically, have led to a one-third reduction in the ration of fish per capita in the area.[7]

The development of large hydraulic infrastructures has not only affected fishing in rivers and lakes, but also in seas. In the case of the Nile, the Aswan High Dam, besides causing the extinction of 30 of the 47 species of fish in the river, has also caused a 90 per cent drop in the catch of sardines and anchovies in the entire Eastern Mediterranean, affecting the lives of thousands of fishing families.[8] Today, we know that these species, like others, spawn in the mouths of large rivers, taking advantage of the massive continental nutrients from the spring river floods. This phenomenon of fertilisation of coastal platforms is more important in enclosed or substantially enclosed seas, like the Mediterranean, which are poor in plankton. A similar impact occurred in the Sea of Cortez (Mexican California) with the deviation of the Colorado River to irrigate the Imperial Valley and the urban development of Los Angeles and San Diego in the USA.[9]

Finally, in addition, the disruption and alteration of natural river flows is causing a crisis for traditional forms of agricultural production that are linked to flood cycles. In Nigeria, the Bakalori Dam caused a 53 per cent loss of traditional crops from the floodplains that were dependent on natural flood cycles; it also ruined livestock grazing and affected the aquifers, vital reserves in drought situations.[10] A report by the World Commission on Dams mentions similar cases in the Senegal River, with nearly 800,000 farmers affected; in the Sobradinho Reservoir (Brazil), with about 11,000 farming families affected; and in the Tarbela and Kotri Dams in Pakistan.[11] In all these cases, as well as in many others, the transition to supposedly more efficient forms of production (by modern irrigation) has resulted, paradoxically, in serious food problems. This has happened because there have not been sufficient means and time given to the transition processes to mature and to be recognised by the communities involved.

Despite their seriousness, these impacts are not reflected in official economic statistics because many of these foods are aimed at local markets and domestic consumption, not entering main retail circuits. It is often argued that these traditional models of production, those linked to the river cycles and traditional fishing techniques, are inefficient. However, when taking into account the environmental and social values at stake, and assuming objectives of sustainability and effective access to food by the poorest and most vulnerable communities, this alleged inefficiency represents high levels of eco-social efficiency.

In this sense, the increasing deregulation and liberalisation of agricultural markets have contributed to accelerating the crisis in traditional forms of production, which, from an environmental and social standpoint, are considered as good practices worthy of protection. This practice causes the destruction of traditional rural structures and increases the migration of millions into the poor suburbs of large cities.

Other Socio-economic Impacts

The crisis of the aquatic ecosystems and other associated phenomena, such as the problems of forests, have an important socio-economic impact, in terms of their effects on a complex set of values, functions and environmental services of great importance.

One of the main causes of the degradation of freshwater bodies lies in deforestation and uncontrolled expansion of the so-called 'farming and cattle-breeding boundary'. Cutting down millions of hectares of primary forest, under the combined pressure from timber, agricultural (generally related to exports) and rancher interests, often leads to the impoverishment of soil, followed by the phenomena of erosion, reduced infiltration into aquifers and a significant increase in run-off. This increasing rate of drainage and the reduction of water retention capacity in the land lead to the reduction of water reserves during summer time and to increased vulnerability during droughts. On the other hand, the channels get clogged by the sediments caused by erosion, thus increasing the risk of flooding downstream.

One of the more fragile and valuable environmental services provided by continental aquatic ecosystems is the regeneration and depuration of discharges. Rivers, and in particular wetlands, are natural depurators that regenerate water quality. When we destroy the life pyramid of its inhabitants, we also damage the river's ability to biodegrade waste, thus deteriorating the quality of these water bodies. One of the most common degradation phenomena is eutrophication (excess nutrients), which can threaten life in aquatic environments, while facilitating the proliferation of toxic algae and cyanobacteria.

Fluvial inundations, alongside cyclical flooding phenomena, have been important to the ecological balance of rivers and their surroundings, the feeding of alluvial aquifers and the fertilisation of floodplains. Furthermore, flooding areas and wetlands reduce water lanes and the power of flood crests.

Wetlands and aquifers play a key role in the natural regulation of the continental hydrological cycle. For years, the controversial project of a waterway between Brazil, Argentina, Paraguay and Bolivia has threatened the world's largest wetland, the Pantanal, comprising 200,000 km^2 at the header of the Río de la Plata Basin, feeding and regulating the basin. In order to improve navigability and facilitate the transport of minerals and raw materials for export, the river is to be dredged and the wetland drained. Studies prepared for the Inter-American Development Bank estimated that this would trigger the extinction of 600 species of fish, 650 birds and 80 mammals, apart from increasing flood risks and the impact of droughts across the entire basin.[12]

The construction of large dams in the world has not only broken the continuity of river habitats, causing the extinction of species and degradation of fishing, but has also dramatically changed the natural flow regimes and solid fluxes (sediments). The sediments that fed the formation of deltas and compensated the natural processes of subsidence for millions of years, commonly affecting these areas (progressive subsidence by compaction of sediments), are now clogging the dams and reservoirs, while deltaic areas become salinised and collapse below sea level. These phenomena are accelerated by the rise in sea level (due to global warming), which is predicted, in a few decades, to cause serious socio-economic consequences for tens of millions of people.

The silts and sands retained by large dams, especially when located in the middle and lower sections of rivers, are also generating serious problems on beaches. Today we know that most beach sand comes from fluvial solid fluxes rather than the erosive effect of waves.

The case of the Aswan High Dam on the Nile, with its impacts on the Alexandria Delta and the beaches of North Africa, is perhaps one of the most significant. The Woods Hole Oceanographic Institution in Massachusetts estimated that Egypt, in six decades, could lose up to 19 per cent of its habitable territories to the sea, which would force the displacement of 16 per cent of its population.

Another disturbing case is the Mekong Delta. The accelerated deforestation of the river headwaters is causing serious erosion, which increases surface run-off, accelerates river kinetics and accentuates the risk of catastrophic flooding. However, the subsequent retention of sediments in large dams, recently built or under construction, and the large water transfers provided to Thailand, cause serious problems in the delta, paradoxically because of the lack of sediments.

The Complexity of the Values at Stake

As previously mentioned, the key problems of the global water crisis in the world are unsustainability, poverty and a lack of democracy. In this context, the inefficiency of traditional management models forces us to consider new approaches and alternatives. But to do so, we must first consider the values at stake and which ethical categories should be used to rank priorities and to guide management criteria.

Throughout the twentieth century, the supply and demand model dominated, with water being regarded only as a commercial good (marginalising its environmental roles). Because of this, water has been managed by the State, which focused on its productive value (for agriculture, industry and services). The primacy of such values in public policy has led to some water productivity myths that have neglected even the most elementary criteria of economic rationality.

Since the advent of neoliberal ideology, which governs the current globalisation model, this approach tends to highlight resource management, while incorporating new criteria based on the logic of economic rationality from free markets.

Since the appearance of the New Water Culture movement, the traditional model of supply and demand is increasingly questioned and water is now considered as an eco-social asset. Here 'eco' expresses both economic and ecological values. Besides its production values, its environmental, social and economic functions and values are also taken into consideration. This holistic approach promotes a transition from the traditional resource management models to the new ecosystemic management models, which are based on ethical principles of equity and sustainability.

As we understand the need to shift from timber management (resource management) to a more sophisticated approach of forest management (ecosystemic management), the Water Framework Directive (WFD), which has been in force in the EU since the end of 2000, promotes this new ecosystemic approach, establishing the promotion and maintenance of good ecological conditions of rivers, lakes and wetlands as a main objective. The aim is not only to preserve the physical and chemical quality of water as a resource, but also to recover and protect the health of aquatic and riparian habitats. As well as physical-chemical indicators, biological ones are also important, as biodiversity itself can be the best testimony to the quality of the water and the health of aquatic ecosystems.

Despite the consistency of this ecosystemic view, the current pattern of globalisation continues to consolidate the resource management approach, while considering water as an economic good that is divisible, appropriable and interchangeable to manage according to the logic of free markets. Moreover, the conceptual mark of neoliberal mercantilism on the subject of water comes full circle when urban water supply services and sanitation are considered as mere economic services.

The undeniable problems of a lack of transparency, bureaucracy and even corruption, which often affect the public management of water services in the world, have been presented by the World Bank as reason enough to justify privatisation. The worldwide dependence on these basic services, with the corresponding and inescapable willingness to pay, coupled with the growing scarcity of good water quality, has made the sector an attractive business area.

However, assuming the principle of sustainability as the basis for water management from an ecosystemic approach, as the EU has done, requires consolidated public accountability in this matter. The complexity of values and rights, present and future, at issue, along with the impossibility of their divisibility and appropriation, make the market an inadequate and simplistic tool.

The values of social cohesion and equity related to basic services, such as water and sanitation (health, education, public safety, etc.), go beyond market logic. Beyond ideological debates, demanding that the market manage these kinds of intangible values and services that are so integral to human citizens' rights to universal access is like asking for the moon. It is unreasonable to expect the market to solve problems of citizenship cohesion and equity, or that it will guarantee the rights of future generations it is insensitive to.

To sum up, beyond the challenge of sustainability, it is clear that the ethical values involved here require a deeper reflection; first about the roles of water and aquatic ecosystems; and secondly about the values and rights at stake.

To illustrate this idea, it is useful to make the contrast between renewable natural resources such as water and wood. Assuming, for a moment, that we have made peace with nature and were able to extract wood and water without affecting the health of forests and rivers, the challenge would be limited to organising the management of wood and water as resources. I do not think there would be any significant problems in timber management, but there would still be serious social and political problems in terms of water. The key, from my perspective, is that wood gives us utilities that are consistently replaceable by capital goods, allowing us to entrust the management of the market with the relevant regulations: the woodcutter sells logs to the sawmill, which then sells wood to the carpenter, who in turn sells furniture to people. However, the values at stake in the case of water are more complex and in many cases water cannot be replaced by capital goods.

The Ethical Grounds:
The Functions, Values and Rights at Stake

Economic science has conceptually muddied two terms of the Castilian language, inherited from Greek. Aristotle clearly distinguished these two terms: *economía* and *crematística*. According to Aristotle *economía* (economics) was the art of managing household goods effectively, while *crematística* (political economy) dealt with all that could be valued in money and, therefore, could be bought and sold on the market. If, by Aristotle's definition of economics, the term 'household' were replaced by the term 'planet', we would have a good definition of the modern ecological economy.

Forcing a monetary value upon intangible goods (environmental and social), and then managing them according to the logic of the market, often leads to serious errors because not all goods are, or should be, tradeable. Daly reasons thus: 'Some argue that human-made capital and natural capital are mutually replaceable goods so that the idea of limiting factor (for production) is irrelevant. However, I think it is pretty clear to common sense that human-made capital and natural capital are mainly complementary and only marginally replaceable...'[13]

The market approach promoted by the World Bank on basic services on which people's health and lives depend has been shown to be a mistake. Water is certainly a well-defined element: H_2O. However, viewing it as a 'useful and scarce' asset, to be managed by market competition rules, contradicts the most basic ethical principles. Unlike other natural resources, water utilities and functions are related to different ethical rankings. This implies the need to give priority to some uses over others, while in each ranking objectives are found that in many cases cannot even be exchanged for cash. Therefore, water management, as well as life and environment management, goes beyond the simplicity of market logic, requiring specific and appropriate management criteria in the different ethical categories in question.[14]

We should distinguish four ethical categories and their respective priority levels, in line with the European Declaration for a New Water Culture. The individual objectives, rights and duties involved in each category require different management criteria.

- Life-water: water for the basic survival of both humans and other living beings must take priority in such a way that the sustainability of ecosystems and universal access to the basic quota of quality water can be ensured as a human right. The water required to maintain basic productive activities on which the diet of vulnerable communities depends should be included in this category.

- Citizenship-water: water for activities and services of common interest, such as water supply and sanitation in homes, should be ranked second in the field of citizens' rights, with corresponding duties of citizenship.

- Economy-water: water used for productive purposes, over and above the level of sufficiency for a decent life, should be ranked third in relation to the right of everyone to improve their living standards.

- Crime-water: water used for illegitimate productive purposes, which should be illegal (pollutant discharges, abusive extractions, etc.) because of the serious damage they do to society's general interests. Such uses should be made accountable through the strict application of the law.

Life-water

Although somewhat marginal, the UN Committee of Economic, Social and Cultural Rights in 2002 mentioned the need to recognise access to the basic quota of potable water as a human right. Currently, and following a Spanish and German initiative, the UN Human Rights Council has begun seeking a clearer and more forthright statement on this matter and has appointed Professor Catarina de Albuquerque as an independent expert to be involved in the process.

It seems clear that the access to these basic quotas of life-water and to basic sanitation services should be part of human rights, which would demand effective guarantees and a maximum level of priority. In this case, the criteria should not be to maximise efficiency (the main focus of economic rationality), but instead ensure efficacy. We are looking at values and services, and the overall responsibility to guarantee them should fall on the community, that is, on governments and international public institutions.

We must not forget that the 30 to 40 litres of potable water per person per day, which has been suggested as the minimum required for a decent life, represents, for a country such as Spain, only 1.2 per cent of the overall national water consumption. There is no argument that justifies 1,100 million people not having guaranteed access to that quantity of water. An alleged lack of financial resources in order to achieve this is unacceptable for the governments of impoverished countries, and even more so for the governments of wealthy nations and international institutions, such as the World Bank. At the end of the day, the 'public, potable and free fountain, in the square, close to everyone's home' was guaranteed in many countries, such as Spain and Portugal, when they were poor and the World Bank did not even exist. The challenge was not exactly financial, but rather political, in the Aristotelian and noble sense of the term. In short, guaranteeing potable and free water in the main square was seen as public responsibility and an important priority, even before the illumination or the asphaltation of streets and roads, not to mention spending on luxury goods or military expenses.

In terms of life-water the necessary quantity and quality of flows to ensure the sustainability of aquatic ecosystems and their environments should also be included. In fact, even from a strictly anthropocentric view, it is impossible to guarantee our existence and well-being separately from the rest of living beings. Indeed, in this case, we are not talking about 1.2 per cent of water used by society, but of the environmental flows of higher magnitude, as well as significant efforts to avoid spillage, preserving water quality and aquatic habitats. So, considering these environmental flows as life-water on the same priority level reserved for human rights may raise some doubts. However, as we have explained, the main reason that 1,100 million people do not have guaranteed access to drinking water is precisely because of a failure of sustainability. The UN has discussed third-generation human rights: the collective rights of peoples, including the right to peace, land and a healthy environment, which is essentially asking the question if it seems acceptable, from an ethical perspective, that living rivers are something for the rich, and the poor must make do with sewer rivers as a condition for achieving the economic development they dream of. The answer seems clear.

In the EU, the Water Framework Directive sees these basic environmental functions of water as top priority. In fact, the flows necessary to preserve the ecological health of rivers, lakes and wetlands are not considered as 'environmental demands', in possible competition with other 'demands', but rather, by law, a restriction upon productive uses. Only 'drinking water' takes higher priority, even if it rarely puts the sustainability of aquatic ecosystems at risk.

Citizenship-water

Providing domestic water and sanitation services represents a qualitative leap in relation to the public fountain that guarantees those 30 to 40 litres per person per day. On average, about 120 litres per person per day are used in a normal European home, without a garden and swimming pool. This amount of water represents about 6 per cent of the water currently extracted from nature. Today, access to such services is considered a right for all, rich and poor. Therefore, although I understand that it would be inappropriate to consider access to such services as a human right, it is necessary to consider them as the right of every citizen. These rights should be linked to corresponding duties as citizens, unlike human rights, which are not linked to any duty, but accrue simply through being alive.

In conclusion, it is all about managing values to which the market is insensitive, such as equity and social cohesion; values linked to the traditional concept of citizenship of common interest that Aristotle defined as the *res publica*, managed by the community or deemed public responsibility.

Ensuring quality water and sanitation services requires the definition of a complex set of rights and duties where it is essential to conjugate different tariff models that ensure appropriate finance, encourage efficiency and the responsible behaviour of citizens.

In today's complex society, ensuring universal access to quality domestic water and sanitation services, while minimising the ecological impact on aquatic ecosystems, is a major challenge. Tackling it requires promoting individual and collective responsibility and caring attitudes. A lockstep tariff system with rising prices may ensure the recovery of expenses via redistributive social criteria. The first level of 30 litres per person per day could even be free, at least for those below the poverty line. The second level, 100 litres, should be paid at a price that approaches the actual cost of the service. At the third level, the price per cubic metre should clearly be higher. Finally, the fourth level, which would be for luxury uses (gardens and swimming pools), would offer a cross-subsidy from those who consume more to those who find it difficult to pay.

In this case, unlike life-water, where economic logic is out of place, we are proposing financial rationality criteria that do not correspond with market rationality. For example, when buying apples at 1.50 euros per kg, often we are offered 2 kg for less than 3 euros. From the so-called economy of scale approach, we sell cheaper to the good customer, encouraging consumption and increasing business profits. The proposed tariff model, however, is based on the opposite criteria. The goal is not to do good business but to provide a good public service of common interest and universal access.

Economy-water

Most of the flows extracted from rivers and aquifers are not dedicated to ensuring human rights or services of general interest, but are instead for productive activities that are mainly of interest to the producers concerned. Globally speaking, the agricultural sector uses over 70 per cent, while the industrial and service sectors use about 15 per cent. These are activities based on the legitimate aspiration of improving living standards above what could be characterised as a level of sufficiency for a decent life. The right of the rich to get richer is debatable, but this right, even if legitimate within certain limits, cannot be considered as part of human rights or citizens' rights. Therefore, from an ethical standpoint, such uses must be managed according to a third level of priority, after life-water and citizenship-water. In this sense, degrading a river by destroying its biodiversity and endangering its fish, or risking the potability of its flows with the justification of promoting economic development, is immoral.

The criteria of economic rationality should be applied here because the objectives of such uses are economic. Each user should be answerable for the costs of their water provision. In addition to this, in the case of shortages, opportunity costs should also be applied, which is simply the cost of resource scarcity. Ultimately, in the area of economy-water, the need to apply the principle of full cost recovery is necessary, including financial costs (amortisation of investments and maintenance and management costs), environmental costs and the value of the resource itself (if supply is lower than demand), that is, the opportunity cost. In this case, there are no reasons to justify direct or cross-subsidies, in the same way that wood is not subsidised for carpenters, and diesel for transport companies.

The scarcity of life-water leads to humanitarian catastrophes and is therefore unacceptable. The scarcity of citizenship-water (water supply cuts or contamination of urban networks) is the result of serious political failure and should therefore also be regarded as unacceptable. However, water scarcity for economic growth can no longer be understood as a tragedy to be avoided at all costs and financially supported by the public treasury; it should instead be understood as an inescapable reality, sooner or later, to be managed using the criteria of economic rationality. With our unlimited ambition, we make the abundant scarce, we make the planet small, making fresh water from rivers, lakes, wetlands and aquifers a limited resource in the process. We must not forget that scarcity is an inherent feature of any economic good, useful and scarce by definition. It is ultimately about applying criteria of economic rationality to the economic use of water. A use, let us not forget, which is to generate benefits for customers through market relationships that govern the productive activities in which the resource in question is used; even if water is preserved as a public good.

We do, however, need to be clear that not all productive activities are profit-driven. As previously noted, in many poorer communities, certain agricultural activities that require water are essential for the basic food production that those communities depend upon. Such uses must be protected as rights in the field of life-water.

Some economic activities, while lucrative, are worth considering as economic activities of common interest to a certain extent. We refer to those that generate social or environmental benefits, which are normally in society's interest but given little or no value by the market.

Unfortunately, in countries like Spain, the argument of 'common interest' has been so manipulated by those in power that this concept needs to be revised. Traditionally, the statement of common interest has been used to justify large public investments in hydraulic works, the traditional strategies of supply, which today are rather outdated. However, the powerful economic groups that have controlled hydraulic policies continue to encourage, in their own interests, a cultural inertia that does not reflect the common interest of today's society. It is therefore necessary to redefine the concept of common interest to consider current priorities. It is also particularly necessary to discuss the alleged common interest of irrigation, justified by the myth of the role of family farming within the rural environment; it is also necessary to end the demagogic use of the argument of hunger in the world, when what is actually being fed is the markets, which the poor (who are those who are hungry) cannot access.

Today, the relative importance of agribusiness has grown from industrial production approaches, either in large farms or intensive farms that use production under plastic. In addition to this, in countries like Spain, the proportion of farms as a sideline activity has been steadily increasing. In this context, family farm agriculture is far from representative of the sector today.

By identifying at least these three types of farming, we can discern different social values. It is difficult to justify characterising irrigation in agribusiness as an activity of common interest; as it is difficult to understand the common interest of irrigation on farms operated by owners who do it as a sideline activity and who usually do not even live in these rural areas.

It is necessary to establish social and environmental criteria that permit the definition of what kind of operation deserves to be considered of common interest. Those operations that consolidate rural networks, with their corresponding social, cultural and landscape values, or those supporting the achievement of certain environmental objectives, would arguably be of common interest in a society with serious problems of urban congestion. In this sense, it is reasonable to protect the family farms that use irrigation and which implement good agri-environmental practices. However, even from this perspective, it is important to reflect upon how support is given and how to encourage good practice and responsible attitudes. It would be preferable to subsidise these activities directly, rather than provide subsidised water, which is what normally happens. With the same cost to the public coffers, it would encourage more efficient and responsible water use.

Public and Private Management: The Crisis of Governance

In recent decades, the neoliberal strategy of the World Bank and the World Trade Organisation (WTO) has reduced the scope of the public field, opening up more opportunities for private initiative. Under this pressure, traditional state functions, such as that of promoting values of justice and social cohesion, have receded and been deactivated. We are witnessing a gradual process of 'starving' the public institutions because of the idea that money is better placed in the taxpayer's pocket. Any electoral programme with a hope of success must promise tax reductions. Distrust of public services is promoted, and they are characterised as inefficient, untransparent and bureaucratic, while deregulation policies are presented as alternatives of flexibility, modernity, efficiency and economic rationality from an interesting mystification of the free market.

Seen from this perspective, ensuring universal access to services of common interest, such as water and sanitation, health or education (those traditionally seen as citizenship rights) comes to be seen as State interference with the free market. Such services are presented as mere economic services, which should be offered in free competition. In this context, it is assumed that the State must withdraw, citizens must become clients and the services in question should cease to be universally accessible and be available only to those who can afford them. This systematic pressure of deregulation on impoverished and developing countries has dismantled, or at least weakened, already poor public services and social protection policies. Even in developed countries, the so-called Welfare State has been affected. In these circumstances, many weakened public institutions are tempted to privatise their services as a way of easing their financial burden.

The privatisation of the public management of water and sanitation services in major cities of impoverished or developing countries (the major operators are not interested in small towns and rural areas) under pressure from the World Bank has led to rebellion among the poorest people, making these policies fail in many countries (especially in Latin America). International operators themselves admit that this failure has caused a change in their strategies. For nearly two decades, the strategy of these companies (mostly of European origin) focused on the so-called unregulated markets. However, they argue today that deregulation in situations of social and political instability involves risks that are too high. Now, the strategy has shifted towards the so-called reliable markets, such as those emerging in the countries of Eastern Europe, including Russia.

There are three main arguments used to justify these privatisation policies:

- the expectation that the private sector will bring massive investments;

- the efficiency incentives of free competition;

- greater control by service users through the exercise of their rights as clients.

However, as has been demonstrated empirically, large private operators have invested little of their own capital in the basic infrastructures of developing countries. This was demonstrated by the PRINWASS research project, developed with EU funding, which assessed the processes of privatisation in various countries.[15] In Argentina, the country where privatisation of urban water management in Latin America began (excluding privatisation during the Pinochet regime in Chile), the investments made remained mostly public and only a small fraction was made by operators, who were given service concessions. This business strategy has always been considered too risky and unprofitable to make massive investments in basic infrastructures. In most cases, the privatisation process only unlocked World Bank loans, which became managed by private operators, although they were charged to the country's public debt.

The argument about the benefits of free competition in other services may be valid, but in this case are not, because it is a 'natural monopoly'. In effect, the privatisation process promotes competition options 'for the market', but not competition 'in the market'. This means that the most we can hope for is short-lived competition for contracts awarded by public tenders (when there is not a direct award). Once awarded, the service becomes managed as a private monopoly for many decades and any rescission or revision of terms is very difficult.

In this context, paradoxically, what usually happens is that there is a reduction in the real level of competition. Indeed, under public management models at local or regional level, contracts for new technologies, maintenance, upgrades and so on are usually contracted from the market, where many specialised small and medium-sized companies compete. It is what is known as the 'market of secondary inputs', which typically produces a significant turnover. However, when the service is allocated to large operators, the 'market of secondary inputs' is usually shielded from competition to the extent that these companies have their own resources. The final result is, paradoxically, less market competition.

The argument of citizens controlling the operator through their rights as clients does not work in this case either, as these rights are only exercised when they can change providers, which is not an option in this case because of the natural monopoly.

The market transparency that is supposedly gained, as opposed to the lack of it in public management, is more a myth than a reality. The fact that public management is often bureaucratic and untransparent does not mean that it has to be like this, nor is private management necessarily more transparent. In fact, if management is public, citizens can demand transparency, whereas private companies are legally protected by the right to privacy of information.

The problems of administrative lack of transparency, bureaucracy, and even corruption, are not solved by privatising public management but by making it more democratic. No one, for example, would propose privatisation as a solution to police corruption. In fact, in countries where these problems seriously affect public life, using private operators, far from solving problems, has fed again the logic of the systems that welcome them. Logically, the most serious ethical and political problems emerge in situations of poverty, to the extent that changing from being a citizen to becoming a client means losing basic rights that the market does not recognise or does not have to recognise.

Today, even in advanced democracies, it is the challenge of promoting public service reforms that promotes participatory management and ensures transparency. Where competition is not possible in the market, it aims to promote competition through information and public contrast between similar services: this is known as benchmarking. For this, the action of an appropriate regulator is necessary at higher levels, to audit and force local and regional operators to publish understandable and comparable data so that various services can be compared.

The words of Vinod Thomas, director of the World Bank in Brazil, are particularly appropriate here: 'When there is a risk that privatisation might create a monopoly, it is better to leave the services in State hands.'

When dealing with such a contentious issue as this one, it is necessary to refine relevant concepts. Often the terms deregulation and privatisation get confused. Assuming public responsibility as a starting point for this kind of service, among many other options, there is the possibility of a concession for its management under proper regulation that ensures effective public control. However, regulating and controlling the management of large operators is difficult and not the sole preserve of governments that choose to privatise their services. On the other hand, if the powers are local, as in Spain, the disproportionate power of these multinationals in contrast to the financial weakness of the municipalities favours the phenomenon known as 'buying the regulator'. In any event, neither in the past or today has the World Bank supported the promotion of the appropriate measures of regulation in its privatisation policy.

Deregulatory pressures, operating both globally and in the European region, merit comprehensive and thorough public debate. In the case of countries that signed the Aarhus Convention, the debate is inevitable if we apply the concept of proactive citizen participation, established by that convention. The decision to privatise these kinds of services should not be taken as a simple administrative matter in offices. Even debate at municipal or parliamentary meetings is insufficient, because these decisions affect citizens' rights and even human rights for several decades. Broad public debate is necessary, which may culminate in a referendum, as recommended by the European Declaration for a New Water Culture.

Today, beyond the formal recognition of the public domain over waters and aquatic ecosystems, we need primarily to think about the challenges posed by the new paradigm of sustainability, then about the obligation of guaranteeing access to potable water, as a human right and, thirdly, about the need to develop global citizenship rights, which include domestic water and sanitation services.

Adhering to principles of inter- and intra-generational equity in water management reinforces the need to reconsider public or European Community management of water ecosystems and aquifers, based on new approaches that ensure the priority of their life functions and the rights of future generations. At the same time, we must face the challenge of ensuring basic rights of citizenship, encouraging responsibility by participation, transparency and accountability, which requires designing and developing new models of public participatory governance.

The serious conflicts caused by privatisation processes strike at the heart of this problem; however, this does not mean that the problem of how to effectively manage these basic services has been solved. Even within the movement for public participatory governance under social control, the debate is open on how to achieve the necessary balance between rights and duties, especially in relation to the financial management of these services. The tariff policy to be implemented is, at the very least, controversial. Understanding and accepting that citizenship rights must be inextricably linked to corresponding citizen duties requires a remarkable cultural and socio-political shift. Such a change cannot be achieved by decree, but requires an extensive process of education, awareness and citizenship responsibility that can only be achieved through new models of participatory governance to make democracy something more than simply voting every four years.

Translated by Joana Maltez

Notes

1   C. Magallón, *Pioneras españolas en las ciencias* (Madrid: CSIC, 2004).
2   Fundación Nueva Cultura del Agua (ed.), *Declaración Europea por la Nueva Cultura del Agua* (Zaragoza: FNCA, 2005).

3   International Center for Living Aquatic Resources Management, Consultative Group on International Agricultural Research, *From Hunting to Farming Fish* (Washington DC: World Bank, 1995). [ICLARM is now renamed The WorldFish Center.]

4   P. Arrojo, *La Nueva Cultura del Agua del Siglo XXI* (Zaragoza: Icaria, Tribuna del Agua-Expo-2008, 2008).

5   M.T. Hill and S.A. Hill, 'Summary of Fisheries Resources and Projects in the Mekong River', presented at the seminar: Mekong: International Seminar for Sustainable Development Through Cooperation, Washington DC, November/December 1995.

6   See J.N. Abramovitz, *Aguas amenazadas, futuro empobrecido: el declive de los ecosistemas de agua dulce* (Bilbao: Worldwatch Institute, 1996); P. McCully, *Ríos Silenciados: Ecología y Política de las Grandes Represas* (Argentina: Proteger Ediciones 2004); publ. in English as *Silenced Rivers: The Ecology and Politics of Large Dams* (London: Zed Books, 2001).

7   Abramovitz, *Aguas amenazadas*.

8   McCully, *Silenced Rivers*.

9   S. Postel, *Reparto del agua: seguridad alimentaria, salud de los ecosistemas y nueva política de la escasez* (Bilbao: Worldwatch Institute, 1996).

10 McCully, *Silenced Rivers*.

11 World Commission on Dams, *Dams and Development: A New Framework for Decision Making* (London: Earthscan, 2000).

12 Fundaçao Centro Brasileiro de Referencia e Apoio Cultural and World Wildlife Fund, *The Paraná-Paraguay Waterway: Who Pays the Bill?* (Executive Summary of the Fundaçao Centro Brasileiro de Referencia e Apoio Cultural CEBRAC) and World Wildlife Fund (WWF) (Brazil: CEBRAC and WWF, 1994).

13 H. Daly and R. Goodland, 'Environmental Sustainability: Universal and Non-negotiable', *Ecological Applications* 6, 1996, pp. 1002–17.

14 P. Arrojo, *El reto ético de la nueva cultura del agua: funciones, valores y derechos en juego* (Barcelona: Paidós, 2005).

15 Prinwass, Research Project financed by the EU (2004). See http://www.ox.ac.uk/-prinwass/es/argentina.shtml.

The Environmental Crisis and the Future of Agriculture

JOSÉ LIMA SANTOS

What possible future (or futures) might there be for agriculture, given the current environmental crisis? Fully answering this question is obviously an impossible mission. At best, I will only be able to contribute here an outline of the answer. It's not only about biology. Biology and other natural sciences have their limitations when it comes to responding to these types of very broad issues. All those sciences that need to be summoned to find an answer, be they natural or social sciences, have some kind of difficult limitations. In addition to this, the effort of an interdisciplinary dialogue, such as is needed to respond to these very broad and multifaceted issues, is in itself a challenge as significant or more so than the limitations we are confronted with in each area.

I will begin by exploring, in some detail, the nature of the problems we face ahead. It seems important to begin here, and not by hurriedly discussing the possible solutions. I'm not going to begin analysing how technology, the markets or public policy can help us solve the problems of agriculture and the sustainable use of land. Rather, I will go back a little and spend (or gain) some time trying to better understand the nature of these problems. When I mention the nature of the problems, I'm not necessarily referring to the objective facts and the natural-scientific knowledge we have of them. I'm mainly interested in understanding how those who are going to decide on the solutions (the public decision makers and, in a democratic society, one way or another, all of us) perceive the problems that their decisions aim to resolve. As was quite rightly underlined by Max Weber, the social agents do not base their decision on the objective context of the action, but rather on the way they subjectively perceive this context. In other words, we're not trying to solve objective problems that arise ahead; we ourselves define the problems.

Also, what is true for the action of each individual is also true, in this case, for collective action and public decision making. In this sphere, problems are constructed intersubjectively. It is in the definition of the problems that we collectively perceive the opportunities and limitations of each context. It is in this exploration of the opportunities and limitations of the context that we learn what we really want (that is, our objectives) and how we're going to try to achieve this (that is, the solutions).[1]

Regarding agriculture problems and the sustainable use of land, I will start by discussing a recent historic transition in the way we, especially in Europe, have been changing our perceptions of these problems. And here, it is not just the objective context that has changed, but also, and mainly, the way in which we have come to perceive it.

Only then will I move on to the second issue, which is the exploration of technological (im)possibilities. On this point it is important to understand to what extent technology will or will not be prepared to resolve the problems of agriculture and sustainable land use.

My third topic has to do with policy tools. What is at stake here is how we can change the human behaviour that needs to change to solve our agriculture and sustainable land use problems. There are many ways to change behaviour: one can prohibit, oblige, criminalise, tax or create markets where they do not yet exist. You can do a lot of things, but what we are ultimately trying to do is change the relevant human behaviour.

So, then, I address first, social perceptions of the nature of the problems of agriculture and sustainable land use; secondly, technological possibilities; and thirdly, policy tools.

1. Changes in our Perceptions of Agricultural and Land Use Problems

It is possible, since the 1980s, to identify two distinct periods regarding our perceptions of the main land use dilemmas we face. First, from the 1980s until the middle of the first decade of the twenty-first century, in Europe, the countryside and rural areas started to be seen as multifunctional, post-productive spaces for leisure, nature conservation and consumption rather than for production. Land was seen as part of quality of life in predominantly urban societies. Secondly, especially from 2007 onwards, global food (food prices crisis), energy (energy prices crisis, renewable energies and biofuels) and ecological (climate and biodiversity crisis) risks, all interrelated with land use, led us increasingly to perceive land as a scarce, fragile and irreplaceable global resource that we depend on for food, energy and ecological security; land as quality of life became land as an essential resource for our lives and survival.

How could this very significant shift in our most basic perceptions of the economic and ecological terms of the land use debate take place, in just five years? Certain economic factors played an important role in triggering this change in perceptions. Let's see how.

1.1. Land, its Use and the Landscape as Quality of Life –
a Multifunctional, Post-productive Countryside (1980s–2003)
This vision of land and countryside (rural space) use has a lot to do with Europe's post-war economic success concerning the general increase in the population's quality of life, as well as the growth in productivity and production of the farming sector.

The history is well-known:

- wealthier people with more time for leisure became more concerned about their quality of life;

- the environment and, in particular, the quality of rural countryside, its natural richness, its cultural weight and its recreational potential (the so-called rural amenities) became valuable assets;

- not forgetting that *environment as quality of life* was one of the most powerful arguments in favour of the existence of a common environmental policy since the Paris Summit in 1972;

- food security was no longer an issue that needed to be resolved, after the success of productive post-war farming (and, if necessary, we could always import our food from an expanding world market);

- modern agriculture was, on the other hand, destroying the quality of the countryside and rural space only to produce more *food surpluses*, which were unable to find distribution in the market.[2]

- there was also a surplus of people in rural areas, particularly in the poorer rural areas that depended the most on farming jobs, due to the success of modern farming, a decrease in labour needed and the increasing mechanisation of agriculture;

- additionally there was *land surplus*, especially in the more marginal areas from a soil fertility perspective, as modern farming managed to produce sufficient food in the more fertile areas; this led to the emergence of the *land abandonment* problem;

- within this context, new functions for the leftover land were sought, in terms of the quality of the countryside, natural richness or cultural significance, either for new residents or visitors to the rural areas;

- this way, part of the rural space, which was initially a space used for food production, was transformed into a multifunctional space for consumption by the new urban middle classes.

1.2 Land as a Scarce, Fragile and Irreplaceable Resource That We All Depend On

The vision described in the previous part is very much a European and more developed countries' vision – the rural space, land and the countryside were seen as something our quality of life depended upon. The food problem was resolved, the essential goods assured, and therefore what we wanted more and more in this context was better quality of life. During this decade, with the turn of the millennium, and especially since 2003 to 2005, a series of events began to develop on a global scale that started convincing us that even for us Europeans, land is not just a part of our well-being – it's much more than that. This sequence of events revealed themselves in the shape of a real crisis with the increase in the price of food in 2007 and 2008.

Between 2005 and April 2008, the world was surprised by dramatic and sustained increases in the prices of cereals and food in general. These increases inverted a long-term declining trend of the prices of cereals in real terms, which had been taking place since the beginning of the 1970s. Food riots among the poorest people on the planet were headlines in the news and were covered on the front pages of the daily press – biofuels were contested and cheaper and more accessible food was demanded. The impact of the price of cereals was particularly negative for the poorest people in the poorest countries as they were already spending most of their budgets on less processed foods (cereals and related items). For these people, the higher prices of cereals meant that they had to further tighten their belts.

Why this rise in prices? How do we interpret this sign? The increase in prices was linked to very low levels of global cereals reserves, resulting from seven (out of eight) years where the harvest of cereals was insufficient to cover global consumption. Just before the 2007 harvest, we had a level of world cereals reserves that could only cover less than two months of global consumption; in other words: if there had been no production that year, it would only have been possible to maintain the usual consumption for two months and then the stocks would have been finished. The level considered safe in terms of the cereals market is a global pre-harvest stock level that allows for a coverage of 100–120 days' (in other words, about four months') consumption at the usual rate. The insufficient production during seven (out of eight) years and the low levels of global stocks led to a growing concern regarding our global capacity to continue to feed the world.

Two alternative explanations for the peak in the prices of cereals arose. One of these, put forward by the Organisation for Economic Cooperation and Development and the UN's Food and Agriculture Organisation in their *Agricultural Outlook 2008–2017*,[3] is based on the importance of a conjuncture of factors, such as the drop in production and droughts in some of the major cereal-exporting countries (Canada and Australia) and the entry of speculative capitals into the cereals futures markets. The FAO and the OECD predicted that in response to the high prices of cereals, farmers from all over the world would decide to increase cultivated areas and invest more in productivity. Production would increase and prices would go down. Summarising, high prices are, in the short term, the most efficient enemies of high prices; in other words, the market adjusts and rebalances itself.

Despite this forecast of a decrease in prices in the short term, the FAO and the OECD also predicted (1) the increase in demand for farming raw materials and biofuels, (2) the expansion of consumption and changes in eating habits in the large emerging economies and (3) that the high price of petrol would, in the medium term (2008–17), lead to higher cereals prices than in the previous decade. They hoped, however, that the growth in land productivity, following the historic trend, would allow for a return to a decrease in the real price of cereals before 2017. The *Outlook* admitted that the growing scarcity of water resources or climate change could create other scenarios, whereby the real prices would not return to the historic decrease. However, these scenarios were neither described nor discussed in detail.

The recent fall in the price of cereals appears to confirm the *Outlook*'s analysis regarding the short term – although the current economic-financial crisis probably provides a better explanation. Regarding the medium to long term, only the future will tell.

An alternative account of the peak in the price of cereals,

defended, for example, by Lester Brown, from the Earth Policy Institute, sees the increase in the price of cereals as a symptom of the global environmental crisis. Analysing the factors that explain the growth of the global production of cereals (which permitted the sustained reduction in the respective prices over the past five decades), Brown concluded that the threefold increase in the global production of cereals was based on the generalised adoption of new varieties of high-yield cereals combined with a threefold increase in irrigated areas and elevenfold increase in the global use of fertilisers – a combination of transformations frequently referred to as the 'green revolution'.

According to Brown, things are currently changing and farmers are faced with a reduction in water availability; less and less response in yields to the use of fertilisers; increases in temperature; loss of cultivated land due to desertification and urbanisation; growing costs of fossil fuels and, mainly, fewer and fewer reserves of new technologies for an immediate growth in land's productivity. Simultaneously, farmers are confronted by a rapid increase in the demand for farming products. Feeding a growing world with decreasing natural resources is really a monumental challenge.[4]

In two very persuasive books Brown tries to convince us that the increase in the price of cereals is just a small tremor warning us of the arrival of the big earthquake.[5] He states that it is the food and not the energy issue (nor any others involved in the current environmental crisis) that is the weakest link (and therefore the first one to break) in the conflicting interrelated connections that link our economic system to the biosphere. What are the main arguments that he uses? One of them has to do with water. In the most populated regions of the world such as China and India, the fact is that we have reached a level of extraction of this resource that leads groundwater levels to drop several metres, on a regional level, while some of the main rivers in these regions no longer reach the sea during the dry season. Therefore, water is a crucial problem, so much so that the cost of farming production has expanded in recent decades in many regions across the world based on expansion of irrigated areas.

Another crucial problem, and the public in general is less aware of this one, is that farm produce is responding less and less effectively to fertiliser addition. This has to do with the architecture of the improved varieties of plants on which we based the increases in yields during the last century. Genetic improvements that we have induced on cereals up until now have not substantially increased the rate of photosynthesis – what they do is to concentrate a larger amount of photosynthesis production in the grain.[6] Therefore, we redesigned the plant so that an important part of what was produced goes to the useful part that we want to harvest: the grain. Well, this change in architecture has limits because the plant also needs to have roots to absorb water and nutrients and needs to have leaves in order for photosynthesis to occur. According to Brown, what is happening now is that we are reaching these limits. The most interesting indicator he mentions is the fact that, in a series of contests in the USA, the yield records of corn (under optimised, irrigated cultivation conditions) are no longer being beaten. This means that we are probably reaching the limits of the technological model that was at the basis of the green revolution, which, we recall, has led to a triplication of the world production of cereals since 1950.

Another important argument is the rise in temperatures. There are many models to estimate the effect of global warming on agricultural production, at various latitudes in many regions across the globe (positive or negative depending on the region). Brown is of the opinion that the effect will be very negative.

The fourth argument has to do with the loss of soil. Here not much argument is needed. We all know that desertification and impermeabilisation resulting from the construction of cities and roads are making us lose fertile soil at a very alarming rate.

The growing price of energy is another of Brown's important arguments. To understand our current food production system we need to understand that, although the food produced contains essentially solar energy from photosynthesis, the production of this food consumes, directly and indirectly, an increasing amount of oil and other non-renewable energies, in the form of fuels and machinery, fertilisers and pesticides (all of which are produced by industry, using very high levels of fossil energy). We also consume energy from the sun but for each megajoule of solar energy that we consume, we spend many megajoules of fossil energy. Therefore, while it is true that nowadays we could produce sufficient food to feed the world's population, it is also true that the growing scarcity of fossil energies may affect our capacity to feed the world. The idea that food production and hunger problems are due to a problem of unequal distribution of incomes (which they obviously also are) is just a part of the reality. There is also the technological problem involved: the green revolution that resolved the food problem for us also left us very dependent on cheap oil to produce the quantity of food we need. We can therefore see that the food crisis and the energy crisis are very much linked: the rise in prices of oil and food in the future will be far from a coincidence. On the other hand, the rise in oil prices has led to new sources of energy such as biofuels, which also contribute (through soil occupation) to an increase in the price of food.

Another of Brown's arguments is about the shrinking backlog of available technologies, where we seek new technologies to solve new problems – there, where the technological promises lie – and find we have fewer and fewer tools, fewer and fewer unused solutions. This is a very debatable idea and one of Brown's weakest ones. This is where the technology optimists turn things around, claiming that technological innovation is *not* a warehouse where we can find resources and where the only thing that is stored for future use is what we have not yet used. After all, we human beings have the creative capacity that has, in the past, resolved many problems that we thought were impossible to solve and therefore the image of a warehouse is a bad metaphor to describe the role of technology.

Finally one of Brown's arguments that I believe is most decisive is about demographic growth and change in diets. Demographic growth is responsible for an annual increase of 70 million mouths to feed – in other words, we will have a total increase of nearly 9 billion people to feed by the middle of this century. What is even more dramatic, but less evident, is that people are changing their diets and that has a much greater effect than 70 million more inhabitants every year. You only need one example. A well-fed Chinese or an Indian vegetarian consumes directly or indirectly about 200 kg of cereal each year. An American consumes, directly or indirectly, 800 kg. An American consumes far fewer cereals directly than an Indian: just 100 kg a year; the remaining 700 kg are consumed by animals for the animal produce (meat, milk and eggs) that he consumes, revealing the low efficiency of animal production as an energy converter. This way, the average American requires an area of productive soil for the production of cereals that is four times larger than the area needed for the average Chinese or Indian. Therefore, the change from vegetarian diets to more carnivorous diets may have a greater effect on the consumption of cereals than population growth. When the average Chinese or Indian changes to a diet similar to an average American's, it is as if there were three more people on Earth. Each person who changes to a similar diet has an effect equivalent to the birth of three more virtual people. We say that we will have 3 billion more inhabitants in 2050 (an increase of 50 per cent), but in terms of cereal consumption, taking into account the increase of virtual people, the increase will be far greater. This is a very important fact because if 30 million poor vegetarians change diet each year then we will have an effect equivalent to more than 90 million new virtual inhabitants; in other words, more than the annual demographic growth (70 million). Here there is a hidden factor that must be considered when seeking solutions: the possibility of adjustments in diet.

In this second explanation (Brown's) of the recent peak in the price of cereals, the food issue is seen as part of the global environmental crisis. In this context, land use in Europe (or in any other region) should not be analysed on its own – analysis should be based on global land use, because it is at a global level that land is limited. In a global market framework, the global limitation of land leads to decision making regarding its use, in Europe, for example, that can have a strong impact on land use in another part of the world. For example, if we, in Europe, want more extensive farming that preserves biodiversity, ecosystems and water and if simultaneously we want to maintain our current levels of food consumption, this can have a very negative ecological effect on other parts of the globe. The product to be consumed in Europe will have to come from somewhere and it is very likely that it will come from somewhere where it is produced at a higher environmental cost and in a less sustainable way (using deforestation for example) than if it were produced in Europe.

Another well-known example is biofuels.[7] Europe wanted to increase its target for the incorporation of biofuels in the transport sector to 10 per cent by 2020. This target, which could only be met if about 50 per cent of raw materials were imported, would have a dramatic effect in terms of increasing cultivated areas in other parts of the world (essentially in the Latin American and African tropics), where the destruction of biodiversity (deforestation) would probably be considerable. It would also put pressure on the price of food in other parts of the world. These effects were considered significantly drastic and therefore Europe began to rethink things. One of the solutions which has been evaluated is the certification of the imported raw materials used to produce the biofuel, to guarantee that they were not going to be produced on recently deforested land. This way, there would be no direct stimulus to deforestation. However, it's easy to see that this does not resolve the problem at all, because the raw material would be produced in areas where a specific agricultural product is currently being produced – for example meat, that was produced on pastures that are going to be converted into land for the cultivation of raw materials for biofuels. As the demand for meat that was previously produced in that area continues, where is it going to be produced now? Probably on new pastures resulting from deforestation. Therefore, the demand for raw materials, even certified ones, will have exactly the same impact on deforestation. Even if a whole country like Brazil were to guarantee that they would not destroy the forest for its certified production of biofuels, other countries would do so, taking advantage of the potential market created due to the decision taken by Brazil. It's very difficult to guarantee sustainability restrictions, in this context, where the markets channel the pressure of the existing demand to a global level. We cannot expect to continue with our current levels of animal product consumption, increase the production of raw materials for biofuels and preserve the forest at the same time, because the area of land available for these purposes is the same. We need to choose what we want.

Another example of unintended effects of decisions taken in one country on the global use of land through globalised markets is production and consumption levels in the state of Massachusetts in the USA. In an article entitled 'The Illusion of Preservation', Berlik et al. show the consequences of the state of Massachusetts – that has one of the highest per capita levels of timber consumption in the world – having decided not to carry out timber exploitation of its significant forested area.[8] The state has an extensive forest area with good timber productivity resulting from the regeneration, over more than a century, of farming areas that were abandoned during the nineteenth century. It regenerated into a broadleaved forest with some natural, scenic and recreational interest. According to local understanding, the forest must be preserved and used as a consumption space, and should not be used for the extraction of timber. As the per capita use of forest products in that state continues to be one of the highest in the world and because it is not covered by local production, it has to be satisfied using imports, frequently from countries that practise much less sustainable forest production than would be the case if the local forest were moderately explored within a context of sustainable forest management. This way, the state of Massachusetts' option is treading a heavy footprint in global deforestation, resulting, after all, from a decision to preserve the local forest – a true illusion of preservation that demonstrates the fact that local uses of land are globally linked by the global markets. The evaluation of the sustainability of a decision, even at a local level, must not be based only on its effects on the use of local land – the effects on the use of global land may well be more decisive in this evaluation.

Therefore, our current perception of land use dilemmas may be summarised as follows: they are about conciliating the growing demand for food and other materials (such as forest raw materials, energetic materials and biomaterials) with the conservation of biodiversity, sequestrated carbon and water, when all these goods result from the use of the land resource, which is globally limited, in a context of global markets that permanently interlink local decisions with the use of global land. They are also, therefore, about managing a scarce resource that is globally limited and fragile – land – to reduce food, energetic and ecological risks. Due to the effects of the global market, this management may only be done with some degree of success if we manage to permanently monitor the effects of our local decisions on the use of soil globally. This is the essential part of an agenda that integrates land use in the more general framework of sustainable development.

2. Technological Promises:
Exploring a Space of (Im)Possibilities

Can technology help us resolve the management problem that has just been defined? Apparently, if we manage to produce more food and other raw materials per hectare, we will need less land to satisfy our needs. In principle, if we need less land the pressure reduces on the natural ecosystems, biodiversity and the remaining natural resources. This way, more intensive farming could be the key to saving more land for nature and for the functioning of essential natural mechanisms.[9]

It's a fact that, due to the increasing pressure of our demand for food, pastures, energy, timber products and other biomaterials, if we define farming intensiveness as production per hectare, this farming intensiveness may be the key to avoid an additional conversion of natural habitat areas into farmland in any part of the world. Nevertheless, up until now, the way in which we have increased production per hectare of land has generally depended on increases in the per hectare use of certain inputs, such as fertilisers, pesticides, water or energy. These increases in the levels of input use per hectare have generally led to less efficient input use. This promoted the existence of unused input surpluses, later emitted in the form of pollutants (the nitrates and phosphates and the eutrophication and pollution of water); it also generated a series of other environmental problems (destruction of food chains by persistent toxic pesticides; reductions in water flows to ecologically critical levels; or increased greenhouse gas emissions). On the other hand, the inefficient use of inputs leads to higher costs and, therefore, less economic competitiveness.

It therefore seems crucial that we must, as far as possible, separate the increase in production per hectare from per hectare input use. This would allow us to become simultaneously more competitive in economic terms and more environmentally sustainable. The extent to which this decoupling of yields and input use is possible is still an open question and there are certainly limits in this technological strategy that promises win-win solutions. These limits are strong, in the short term, and are generally associated with technological lock-ins; for example, the full expression of the genetic potential of the genetically improved cultivated plants that we use now depends on simple ecosystems (reduced competition with other species but also reduced protection against predators and other auxiliaries, and therefore the increasing need for pesticides) and abundant levels of water and nutrients in the soil. These varieties were systematically selected for this type of agro-ecosystem and this is what makes it difficult to do without high levels of inputs (pesticides, nutrients, water and energy) per hectare without losses in production. This resistance to change in the agroecosystem shows the relevance of a technological-model approach: there's no point trying to change an element of the system; innovation won't work unless we innovate the whole system. In the long term, however, the reorientation of genetic improvements towards more robust and resistant plants in less artificial agroecosystems, along with other innovations generated in other areas of agronomic research, may change many things. This is the promise of technology.

There are at least two technological strategies to decouple levels of production per hectare from increasing input use per hectare:

- Increasing the efficiency of input use, applying these inputs in a more precise and targeted manner – a strategy generically referred to as 'precision agriculture'. Its various areas include precision agriculture *sensu stricto*, new irrigation techniques, the integrated protection of crops or minimum tillage techniques.

- Copying and optimising ecological processes that occur in the natural ecosystems (predation, parasitism, symbiotic fixation of nitrogen, mycorrhiza, mixture of annual and perennial crops, covering soil with vegetable material, etc.) to substitute purchased inputs (pesticides, fertilisers, energy and water); what is being discussed here is the creation of agroecosystems whereby the increase in productivity results from better efficiency of the internal functioning of the ecosystem in terms of the material and energy flows.[10]

These two strategies make up the new technological model required to face the new land use dilemmas. This new model will not emerge, however, without a reorientation of agronomic research and, above all, without an increase in the public financing of this scientific-technological research that is currently so underfunded.

3. Changing Behaviour: Political Instruments and Governance

From the discussions in points 1.2 and 2, we can try to find summary lines of action to confront our current land use dilemmas and promote the sustainability of food, agriculture and the use of global land. Some examples include:

- halting desertification (which is particularly difficult in a context of climate change);

- changing the human diet, going down in the food chain;

- increasing the efficiency of animal conversion;

- controlling the urbanisation of land;

- increasing efficiency in water use, in order to be able to expand (or maintain) irrigated areas sustainably;

- reducing the dependency of agroecosystems on fossil energy (which is particularly difficult to equate with the high yields that we need).

Any one of these 'lines of action' implies important changes in our current production and consumption habits, that is, changes in human behaviour. One example of a line of action that seems clearer in terms of the changes in behaviour involved is the following: changes in our diets by moderating the consumption of animal products. Due to the energetic inefficiency of animal production, this change in behaviour will lead, as we have seen, to a decrease in the pressure that our current food consumption habits exert on the land resource.

In what ways can we change the human diet? This is a good question because it reveals the existence of a wide range of options in terms of policy tools, collective action models or governance mechanisms, which also apply, *mutatis mutandis*, to other imposed behavioural changes.

This is also a good question because here we basically know what needs to be done. Here there is no considerable technological uncertainty. We all know that if we had the same diet as the average Chinese or Indian, we could feed 10 billion people on Earth. Here, we know the relevant science. But here there's another type of science required: the science of human behaviour. How do we change human behaviour? I will give you three examples. These examples should be seen as parables that illustrate three more generic types of governance – three types of policy tools.

The first option is the one that is currently most insistently proposed to us: refrain from intervening, that is to say, leave the solution up to the market. What happens if we don't intervene? The problem will end up being resolved. Without sufficient cereals and if we continue to insist on eating meat, the price of cereals will end up increasing. If the price of cereals goes up, the price of meat will rise even more, because, as we have seen, animal production is not very efficient in its use of cereals. If the price of meat rises, we're going to be forced by the market to eat fewer animal products. The problem does indeed resolve itself, by worsening the scarcity of food. The market will manage the scarcity – that's what it's for after all! But in the meantime, with the prices of cereals so high, how many poor 'vegetarians' will be left behind? Leaving the solution up to the market is a possible option, but I don't know whether we will be willing to pay the ethical and geopolitical costs involved – the recent food uprisings and many regional conflicts demonstrate that these issues are not only ethical but also geopolitical.

The second option is to appeal to ethical awareness and common sense. After all it seems that eating too much meat is not that healthy and health statistics demonstrate that an intermediary diet such as the 'Mediterranean' one is superior to a 'carnivore' one. Therefore we can appeal to people's common sense. It makes sense to change diets. A complicated problem is the ethical argument, especially when appealing to the rights of future generations. Why are we so worried about future generations when, apparently, we don't seem that worried about the problem of billions of people currently affected by hunger and undernutrition? (Or, at least, why do we appear to spend so little energy trying to resolve this?) Therefore, appealing to this is certainly important, especially when giving a good example, as some (vegetarians, for example) already do, showing that it is possible to make choices and change behaviours. But how long will it take for ethics to produce significant effects, that is, change behaviour on a significant scale and at the adequate rate? If it takes too long, this will be a solution that, theoretically, is very different from the first (not intervening), but is similar in practice. We will not resolve the problem at all. It will be the market that will resolve the problem, with the ethical and geopolitical costs mentioned above.

But there's a third option, which may be explained using as an analogy the copying and domestication of the ecosystems' mechanisms. In this case, it's not about copying and domesticating natural mechanisms, but rather using market logic to find a solution; that is different to leaving it all up to the market. In the end, it's all about domesticating the market mechanisms. The market provides people with very important information; the price informs us about the scarcity of a good. There's no need for anyone to do any planning or gather data. The product's price on the shelf in the shop automatically transmits this information to people. How can one domesticate market mechanisms to lead to an intended change in behaviour? Could this change diets? For example, taxing cereals used in animal feed (easy to do from an administrative perspective and efficient if adopted on a global level).[11] As long as the tax is sufficiently high, it will have a dual effect: (1) making meat sufficiently expensive that the wealthier moderate their consumption; and, simultaneously, (2) making cereals cheaper for food for the poor 'vegetarians' of this world. This instance is a simple case: not just the science of the problem, but also the policy instrument to be used are pretty clear. More difficult problems arise, of course, in the governance of what would apparently be a relatively simple solution: How to avoid the political backlash from those who are going to lose out (the wealthier, meat consumers and producers worldwide)? How to avoid the impact of the increase in prices of food protein on the poorer populations? How to achieve the simultaneous adoption of this measure in all countries (without which the free-riders will win and the measures will not be effective)? Once again, using this example as a parable (referring to a more general type) and not necessarily as a real case, one could ask whether these difficulties really are insurmountable obstacles in the path of making market mechanisms work for us. On the contrary, they can be seen as clues to transforming practical difficulties into opportunities, through a reflection on the means of governance that can contribute to overcoming them.

Translated by Janette Ramsay

Notes

1 Daniel Bromley, 'Reconsidering Environmental Policy: Prescriptive Consequentialism and Volitional Pragmatism', *Environmental and Resource Economics* 28.1, 2004, pp. 73–99.
2 See M. Shoard, *The Theft of the Countryside* (London: Temple Smith, 1980); and J.K. Bowers and P. Cheshire, *Agriculture, the Countryside and*

Land Use: An Economic Critique (London: Methuen, 1983).

3 FAO–OCDE, *Agricultural Outlook 2008–2017* (Paris: OCDE; Rome: FAO, 2008).

4 Lester R. Brown, *Outgrowing the Earth* (New York: W.W. Norton, 2004).

5 Lester R. Brown, *Plan B 3.0* (New York: W.W. Norton, 2008); and *Outgrowing the Earth*.

6 Brown, *Outgrowing the Earth*.

7 S. Bringezu et al., *Towards a Sustainable Biomass Strategy* (Discussion Paper 163; Wuppertal: Wuppertal Institute for Climate, Environment and Energy, 2007).

8 M. Berlik, D. Kittredge and D. Foster, 'The Illusion of Preservation: A Global Environmental Argument for the Local Production of Natural Resources', *Journal of Biogeography* 29, 2002, pp. 1557–68.

9 R. Green, S. Cornell, J. Scharlemann and A. Balmford, 'Farming and the Fate of Wild Nature', *Science* 307, 2005, pp. 550–5.

10 See S. Scherr and J. McNeely, 'Biodiversity Conservation and Agriculture Sustainability: Towards a New Paradigm of "Ecoagriculture" Landscapes', *Philosophical Transactions of the Royal Society*, Review Issue on 'Sustainable Agriculture', 2006.

11 See Brown, *Outgrowing the Earth*.

Hyper-consumer Society
and Happiness

GILLES LIPOVETSKY

It is widely accepted that we live in mass consumer societies. However, we have to be fully aware that this type of society, which was established in western countries after the Second World War, has now come to an end. Of course, we still use the term 'consumer society' but, in truth, it is no longer the same one that exists today. We live in a new consumer society, as a new phase of capitalist consumption has been put in place. I suggest that this be called 'the hyper-consumer society', and I would like to take this opportunity to present some of its features.

The First Feature

Since the end of the 1970s, the technologisation of households (cars, televisions, telephones, electrical appliances) has spread to three-quarters of our homes in the western developed economies. It was at this time that multi-equipment homes appeared, which meant that, from that period on, more and more homes possessed an increasing number of goods of the same type: more cars, more televisions, more mobile phones (even eight-year-old children own phones nowadays), more cameras, radios, iPods, computers, and so on. Up to then, consumption was organised according to a semi-collective logic, with the core element being the family and each family having a car, a television and a telephone. That has changed. With the hyper-consumer society, it is no longer a semi-collective logic that prevails, but rather an individual one. Nowadays, individuals are equipped with specific products. The traditional consumer society has favoured individualism by means of consumer hedonism in holidays, leisure, media; all of this has had a major effect on traditions, morals and the roles allocated to each gender. Hyper-consumption has pushed this logic one step further, motivating a hyper-individualism that offers individuals greater autonomy in relation to their families, to their schedules and to their use of objects. We now have a de-synchronised, misaligned, personalised type of consumption. We could say, with a slight nod to Marx: to each his own objects, to each his own use of time, to each his own pace. It is in this sense that we are dominated by a hyper-individualistic type of consumption, which is characterised by a life lived profoundly à la carte and a personalised use of objects and services.

The Second Feature

Up to now, consumer behaviour has been established according to specific class cultures. Urban workers, rural workers or the lower and middle classes behaved in accordance with the group to which they belonged: social classes exercising symbolic pressure for consumers to adopt consumer behaviour according to their environment. For example, if a woman bought a pair of shoes or a bag that did not belong to her world, jokes would be made, a certain irony exercised to try to bring her to her senses: 'Who does she think she is?' 'She must think she's rich or something.' There was a certain class conformity that would make individuals act like their peers. This is now tending to disappear. Today, all social groups express their taste in brands, fashion, luxury, tourism, but also in a demand for quality, for standards related to what is natural, young, thin. All these aspirations are no longer specific to one social group; they have become widespread, and the only difference, albeit a major one, is in who has the money to obtain these commodities. Despite this difference, expectations and benchmarks are still the same; they have spread to the whole of society, even if economic inequalities remain profound. However, in people's 'heads', in terms of their aspirations, there is no fundamental difference. We are witnessing the deregulation and disorganisation of class behaviour. Nowadays, consumers spend their money here and save it there. The same woman that buys a skirt at Zara for 50 euros can also buy a bag at Gucci: she mixes and matches. It is no longer frowned upon by her social class and it is even considered quite elegant to be able to mix and match products of different prices and prestige. And in disadvantaged social groups, things are the same. In poorer neighbourhoods, young people want brands; they aspire to trendy products, which they wear in their own way. Class no longer prohibits such a thing. In the past, the working classes used to say 'luxury is not for us'. That is no longer the case. They know all about the big brands and want to have access to them; hence the rise of globalised counterfeiting, which represents 5 per cent of the global trade of luxury goods. Nowadays, everyone aspires to brand ownership, quality and leisure. Consumption is now deregulated and destructured. It follows the same individualistic type of logic that we see in families, sexuality, religion and politics.

As a result, the very significant phenomenon is that consumption follows the same logic as globalisation. Neoliberal capitalism is characterised by what Edward Luttwal calls 'turbo-capitalism', and marked, since the 1980s, by the dismantling of administrative rules. The logic of deregulation also works in favour of consumption, with the former limits, curbs and collective controls on individuals having disappeared. The result is consumers who are ever more nomadic, flexible, fragmented and uncoordinated. It is not a trend; it is the inescapable effect of a consumer logic that is no longer part of a class ethos.

It is within this context that one sees the contradictory expectations of the hyper-consumer emerge. This hyper-consumer primarily wants things free of charge, which is new. Young people download music free of charge; they no longer want to pay for newspapers, magazines and films. This is now a very strong trend and one that jeopardises cultural industries, in particular the record industry; but at the same time the hyper-consumer is attracted to expensive brands. We are living in odd times, because we talk about 'low-cost', while there is a huge increase in the market for luxury goods. We also see a bipolarisation of consumption developing. Extremes cohabit. On the one hand, 'low-cost', and on the other, luxury goods, which have never been so successful.

We have been told that the current global financial crisis will radically change the world of consumption. I don't believe a word of it. If you take the first example that I mentioned, then it is obvious that the future is all about hyper-individualisation: this is a dynamic that will continue, except perhaps in the field of transport, where there will be more public transport. But don't think that people are going to give up their holidays, their iPods, iPhones and laptops. All of these will become even more widespread. As for the second example: We won't be going back to the previous social regulations governing consumption. It is unthinkable in a hyper-individualistic universe. Low-cost will also be part of the future, and not because of the financial crisis. Even people who are not poor shop for low-cost items and services. Why? Because we live in a world of hyper-consumption and we have a permanent flow of new products to buy. We cannot buy everything, so we have to save on some things, in order to be able to buy others. We save a little on pasta and on soft drinks to be able to pay for a trip this summer and go on holiday. This logic is not because of the global recession but it is an integral part of hyper-consumption. It has been said that there is a crisis of luxury goods, but that is practically over. In a recent interview with the leader of the luxury brand, Tod's, he stated that: 'the crisis of deluxe products in Asia is negligible. Actually, business is going very well and in Europe there are overall signs of recovery.' When one thinks of the traders' bonuses, one is not too worried about luxury goods, which is an area with a very good future throughout the world because, currently, there is a very small minority who consume luxury goods. And there are more and more rich people. More and more people aspire to luxury goods, which represent the elusive dream.

The Third Feature

What explains the infernal dynamics of consumption? Why does it never stop? Why is it that from the moment one earns a little more, one wants to consume even more? Why 'always more'? Traditionally, the Veblen model is used to explain this enigma. Basically, according to this model, what pushes the consumer to buy is the desire to show off, to be recognised, to be different from inferior groups, to inspire envy and admiration: essentially, for symbolic profit, status and prestige. It is this model that contains what sociologists, such as Bourdieu, called the logic of distinction. This scheme was already evident in the 1950s. The American sociologist Vance Packard wrote a book entitled *The Status Seekers*, in which he describes the American middle classes with their suburban villas, cars, garages, televisions, and neighbours who came to check you had the right fridge. And people don't buy things for their usefulness, for their use value; they buy them for reasons related to their status, for symbolic purposes.

I think this model has become less relevant. It has not disappeared yet but it is no longer structural or dominant because consumer goods have become widespread in society at large. In today's society, one does not buy a microwave, a fridge, a television, a computer, a mobile phone to stand out from other people. Why does one buy them? For well-being, escapism, communication, experiences; essentially, for pleasure. Today, we are buying more pleasure than status. When you buy a mobile phone, it's basically for making and receiving calls, for sending text messages, listening to music, taking photos. In short, an experiential, emotional gain that is no longer linked to status. I obviously don't deny that there are status-related expenses, in particular in the emerging economies where the many nouveaux riches proudly show off their watches and luxury cars. There are still, and there will always be, ostentatious consumers. However, another type of consumer is emerging; one who bases his spending on the pursuit of sensations, escapism, pleasure, much more than status. Hyper-consumption coincides with the type of consumption that is more intimate than esteem-related, more emotional than status-related.

Here is another similar example. When one talks about consumer obsession, frivolous, trendy and luxury objects often spring to mind. However, there is another area that is often under-estimated and which is booming, that of medical consumption. Everywhere, social security budgets are in the red. We are consuming ever-increasing quantities of medical appointments, medicine, examinations; and this is only the beginning, because the world's population is growing older. We are going to live increasingly long lives and witness increasing levels of medical consumption. I would like sociologists to tell me how one can explain medical consumption from the point of view of the symbolic class competition model! A visit to the doctor is not governed by a logic of esteem, but rather one that is medical and for strictly personal reasons. This increase in hyper-individualistic and post-status-related consumption is one of the major features of the hyper-consumer society.

In more general terms, hyper-consumption works like a trip away somewhere; a moment to breathe, allowing us to experience short moments of pleasure, to escape a little or a lot from the banality of everyday life. Consumption works like an instrument that allows us to fight the fossilisation of our humdrum existence and the hyper-consumer is obsessed with permanently having new experiences. We are obsessed with novelty. We need novelty for new emotions. Baudelaire says somewhere that curiosity has become a fatal passion. Today, it is not intellectual curiosity, of course, but the curiosity of having new experiences: going on holiday, watching a film, listening to music. Something new always has to happen, as if we were worried about repeating the same experience. After all, I think there is something metaphysical in consumption: it is a fight against time. We are searching for a kind of permanent rejuvenation of our experience. The consumer wants to be like the phoenix, which always rises from its ashes. So, I ask the question, once again: What is the reason for this boost in consumerism? There are three major factors involved.

First of all, it has to do with the global competitive economy, which is continuously inventing new products. And since Marx, we have known that it is the object that creates the desire. Desire does not come first. When there were no iPods, we couldn't desire them. We didn't desire computers, when there weren't any. We didn't wish to catch a plane, when there were no planes. There are an increasing number of innovations: the reason behind the infernal advance of consumption. Let me give you some figures. In the 1990s, one hundred new food items were created in the world every single day. A hundred thousand new products are launched in Europe every year. There is a boom of new products and this is what is continuously re-launching consumption.

The second reason is the legitimisation of a hedonistic culture. The consumer society has won. Nowadays, spending money and enjoying life are no longer forbidden. One is no longer dominated by the logic of saving and sacrifice. As we have seen recently, the sub-prime crisis is the consequence of this. On the one hand, there is stimulation and easy credit, which pushes one to buy, and on the other hand, there is an aspiration on the part of consumers to always have something new and experience new things through holidays, leisure, tourism and new products. Tourism has become the prime global industry and this is only the beginning: in a few decades' time, there will be billions of tourists travelling the planet. In effect, the hyper-consumer wants to live now and not later. In the past, the church would say: you should prepare yourself for the afterlife and learn to renounce things, as the Earth is a vale of tears. This culture has been discredited. We want to live our lives to the full because we increasingly believe that there is only one life. And if you only have one life, you want to enjoy it, experience new things and, in a world void of traditions, experience means experiencing buying new things. Hence, the endless advance of consumption.

Thirdly, our hedonistic world is not really hedonistic. We pay a high price for our individualism and hedonism through our levels of anxiety and an increasing feeling of individual malaise. We are an individualistic society, in terms of performance, with less and less stability and institutional sociabilty: suddenly individuals are feeling lonely, extremely unstable, vulnerable and anxious. And what do they do when they are anxious or depressed? In the past, they would go to mass. The churches are now empty. So, all they have left is consumption, which has become the therapy of the hyper-modern individual. Marketing people know that when a woman is depressed, she goes to the hairdresser, buys a dress, goes shopping. Consumption has come to make up for our discomfort. This is an illusion: the unhappiness does not stop. It is the ever-present price of individualisation and the performance demands of capitalism. Individuals try to forget, in order to feel a little better, and consumption is a process that allows us to spend our time, to hide our misfortunes and our different types of dissatisfaction. These are the three factors that underline the frenzy of the hyper-consumer.

The Fourth Feature

No class barriers have been broken down. All the former barriers to consumption are still around. In the past, there was a specific time and place for consumption. For example, in order to go to the cinema, there were specific screenings and one had to go to a specific location. Now, that is no longer the case. You can still go to a cinema but you can also rent a DVD, download a film, or watch a film on your computer, your mobile phone or DVD player. It is possible to watch cinema at any time of the day or night, anywhere at all; there are fewer and fewer spatial/temporal constraints on consumption (with home delivery, cash machines, etc.). One consumes everywhere, on the motorway, in stations, on the underground, at airports. At London's Heathrow, you are not sure whether you are in a supermarket or at an airport. Increasing numbers of establishments open at night. In São Paulo or New York you can go to the gym or do your shopping 24 hours a day. Hyper-consumption is the infiltration of market logic in every place and moment of our lives: we are part of continuous consumer logic. The current financial crisis will in no way change this dynamic, which will increase further with the development of cyber-shopping and electronic consumption. Here, there are no longer limits for the cybernaut; he gives the commands on the keyboard of his computer, wherever he wants, whenever he wants, 365 days a year. There is no limit. And there's more. Hyper-consumption has changed time and the meaning of certain social functions. Let's take the case of feast days (holy days, holidays). In all societies there have been feast days for social, religious and traditional reasons. But consider a feast day, such as Christmas, nowadays: it is no more than a consumer feast day and even hyper-consumer feast day, a veritable consumer orgy. People over-consume because they want to make their children happy, to give themselves a feast, to give pleasure. In its most profound sense, hyper-consumption is the almost wholesale commercialisation of our lifestyles; it is the most intrusive commodification of desires and satisfactions.

Paradoxically, it is at the very time that the virtual, cyberworld is developing that one sees a new type of research into well-being, a more emotional, more sensitive, more qualitative well-being. The material comfort of the 1950s and 1960s, where one bought a car or modernised the kitchen, is no longer enough. Hyper-consumers want to feel good, sense aesthetic emotions and greater quality of life. We no longer live our lives in quantitative terms; we are living with the logic of quality research. I am not saying we will obtain it: it is what one values. Quality of life affects the environment, the air, products, but it also affects urban planning, interiors, gardens, heritage. Everywhere, we are seeking products with a more sensitive or cultural resonance. Look at our heritage, the rehabilitation of towns, the love of things ancient. All of this does not reveal the modernity of the 1950s, in which we eliminated everything that was old. Today, we renovate everything that is old because we have more aesthetic, more emotional demands in terms of our well-being.

One can also see this new search for well-being in design. Compare design in the 1950s, with its Buicks and Cadillacs, with their phallic and aggressive style, with modern Japanese cars, which are round, maternal and soft, and which meet the needs of a consumer in pursuit of emotions and feelings. Just look at the huge success of home decoration. People spend more and more time at home, decorating their apartments to their own specific taste. In the middle of this global recession, we have seen people spending more on terraces, balconies, windowsills. People have taken fewer holidays away and have invested in their homes, giving gardens and plants an escapist value. But look again at the success of massages, saunas, spas, thalassotherapy, Californian hot tubs; everywhere we can find sensory hedonism, an array of sensations which is sought after and valued. We want a better and intimate well-being at the time when the civilisation of the virtual unfolds. We are making life increasingly virtual while experiencing a culture of the senses, a corporification of the senses. A new culture of well-being is developing and the crisis continues.

The Fifth Feature

The hyper-consumer society undeniably presents a blind, devastating, suicidal dimension for humankind in the future. Here is a society that has been built to be indifferent to long-term consequences; a society that has led to ecological catastrophe and one that will jeopardise a part of future generations due to the degradation of the biosphere, the depletion of natural resources and global warming. All this will inevitably lead to less predatory forms of production that will be less damaging to the planet. But we should insist that a more sober economy and a new energy model (energy economies, less fossil fuel energy consumption, post-oil) does not mean the end of the hyper-consumer society. In the long term, it is possible to imagine a future which would, on the one hand, be marked by a decrease in fossil fuel consumption and, on the other, by growth in renewable energy and clean energy consumption. Under these conditions, energy and ecological challenges lead to the sustainable development of the hyper-consumer society and not its disappearance. Ecology, the demand for sustainable development, will not put an end to the hyper-consumer society. It is going to make it possible to have sustainable development compatible with the biosphere and that will be easier as we move towards more service-related economies that focus on services that consume less energy. With the combination of energy-based and increasingly service-driven economies, we are moving towards a new type of society, but one which nevertheless remains hyper-consumerist. And this is because the commodification of needs is never-ending. On the contrary, it will spread worldwide. Try to speak to the Chinese and the Indians about a drop in growth and consumption and they will burst out laughing. They want to be part of the hyper-consumer society and they will be. The exponential commodification of the world is inescapable. What cannot continue is our energy development model. That must change. But such a change will not put an end to the hyper-consumer society.

The only thing that now remains is to assess this hyper-consumer capitalism from a more directly existential viewpoint. How are we going to assess this society in terms of people's happiness? Here, what is clear is that our situation is paradoxical. We live longer and longer, in better health, and we are materially better off. Average working hours have been greatly reduced. Everyone is free to enjoy his or her own sex life. People are free to choose whether they want children or not. We can get married or not. Under these conditions, seen from outside, a Martian could say, 'On this part of the planet, men and women live happy lives.' Seen from within, things are not so clear. In polls conducted over the last thirty years, Europeans have said they are happy: eight or nine out of ten of them say they are either happy or very happy. However, at the same time, there has never been so much anxiety nor so many psycho-pathological problems: depression has multiplied sevenfold in the last thirty years, the use of anxiolytics is on the rise, and suicides and attempted suicides now affect the young. It looks like the polls on happiness do not accurately reflect reality. Nevertheless, when one asks the French: 'Are you happy?' eight or nine out of ten say yes. But if you ask them, 'Do you think that other people are happy?' they answer 'No, they're not.' We find the same type of answers concerning work. Question: 'Are you happy with your professional situation?' Most people say yes. Second question: 'Do you think others can be optimistic in relation to their work?' Answer: 'No, they have a lot to worry about.'

So, let's be careful with polls on happiness. What do we really see? Workers feel threatened by globalisation, intensifying their frustrations in connection with lack of professional recognition and stress, resulting from new performance demands that affect the self-esteem of a number of wage earners. Work is less of a physical strain, one works less, but at the same time there is growing stress resulting from the world of competition, ever higher objectives, and individual loneliness (linked to the decline of class solidarity cultures). Look at the recent succession of suicides at France Telecom. We are not talking about the disinherited, but executives, women and men who had a job. That shows the extraordinary suffering that the contemporary world of professional performance can cause. We can live in the world of well-being but the result is not always extra happiness. The culture of efficiency optimisation is very expensive. Our society has become both softer and harder at the same time. It is no longer possible to think like modern optimistic philosophers, who believe that everything is irresistibly moving in the direction of 'better': more knowledge, more technology, more democracy, more freedom. And more happiness. There is none.

Other areas show the same paradoxes. Bodies and libidos are free. You can act whatever way you like in this area. You will not be judged, unlike in the past, but at the same time sexual misery still exists. In a recent poll in twenty-six countries, more than one person in two, both men and women, said they were dissatisfied with their sex life. There is a true sexual revolution, it's undeniable, and that should bring freedom, as well as greater happiness. But let's be honest, this is not what we see at all.

There is more. Most Europeans say they are happy. But if we ask them the question: 'Are you becoming happier and happier?' The answer would be negative. We consume three times as much energy as we did in the 1960s. Nobody would dare say that they are three times as happy. France's GDP has doubled since 1975 but would anyone dare say the French are twice as happy? The economic dynamics of growth exist but happiness is not part of this growth. In any case, it does not grow at the same pace as economic life.

France is the fifth world economic power, but in terms of polls on happiness it is in thirty-ninth place. The USA, which is 'number one', sits in seventeenth position when it comes to happiness. Once again, we have to look at the polls with a certain caution. But they at least indicate that the level of GDP does not equate with levels of happiness. The hyper-consumer society and the happy society are not synonymous. We live in rich, prosperous societies with a lot of individual unhappiness.

It is within this context that we see new models of happiness emerge. Since the 1970s and 1980s, there have been those who have advocated a non-materialistic happiness. The solution put forward is an internal-subjective revolution, going against the grain of the modern dynamic, which, since Descartes, has promised greater happiness by way of the technical domination of the world. The tenants of the New Age (Buddhism, psycho-corporal techniques, personal development, new spiritualities) denounce the standstills of the Promethean model by giving priority to the return to oneself, to the 'broadening of the consciousness', to the inner work of individuals on themselves. The neo-directors of happiness tell us that we should change ourselves through our consciousness. It is enough to make our thoughts harmonious, to love ourselves in order for us to achieve a happy life. If we learn to love ourselves, we will change our way of thinking and life will become happy. In this type of philosophy, we find the idea that happiness can be learnt and belongs to us: we can become masters of our own happiness. That is what New Age gurus endlessly repeat.

Should one follow these masters in spirituality who sell happiness programmes? I think that they are magical forms of thought that channel a great deal of naivety and false promises, because if there is one thing that the experience of life teaches, it is that we do not possess happiness. We are incapable of becoming masters and possessors of happiness. Rousseau explains it very well by showing that we humans are incomplete beings, unable to suffice each for himself and we are people who need others to know plenitude. It is because happiness is inseparable from rapport with others that the individual is unavoidably doomed to the deceptions and injuries of life. We are relational beings; we live with others and depend on others for happiness. When someone hurts you, when you are worried about your children, when you are having trouble with your love life, you can have a beautiful car and live in a sumptuous mansion but that will not prevent you from being unhappy. Happiness is not automatically connected to the possession of things. We cannot become the masters of happiness, because we rely too much on others and we cannot do without them. That is why happiness comes and goes as it wants and not when I want. That is why we cannot find this perfect happiness that the masters of spirituality teach. We are finite beings and can only strive towards what Rousseau called 'frail happiness', moments of happiness and not a life of perfect plenitude.

I would now like to conclude by highlighting two points. First of all, we can see that, despite our pursuit of the techno-scientific domination of the world, our inability to govern happiness will continue, contrary to the hopes of the Enlightenment. Our power over things increases, but not the power to increase our *joie de vivre*. This modern project of supposedly unlimited power clearly reaches its boundaries here: happiness is not moving forward, it is obstinately escaping human control. Of course, technology, science and democracy have considerable power: that of delaying the major misfortunes of humankind (mortality, malady, great hardships and tyranny). We do not contest this; men have shown they have the power to prevent huge calamities. So, the objective quality of life increases, but the inner, subjective quality of life has come to a standstill. In fact, we are now more able to affect people's hardships than their happiness.

Of course, I have to qualify what I have just said, because the poorest countries are the unhappiest and in rich countries, the people who say they are unhappiest are part of the most disadvantaged classes. In this sense, we can cite the proverb, 'Money doesn't necessarily make us happy, but it certainly helps.' Material well-being does not bring happiness but 'it does help a little'.

However, having said that, only part of the proverb is true. In effect, the polls reveal that, from a certain point of view, when one becomes richer, one does not become happier. If your salary is 40,000 dollars, if you earn 20 per cent more, you will not be 20 per cent happier! When you have nothing, material well-being can bring true happiness but, after a certain point in life, it is no longer true. Once again, progress in terms of consumption and GDP does not mean progress in terms of happiness. After a certain threshold, having more money, consuming more, does not afford more happiness.

The second and final point: I have already underlined a certain number of aspects of the hyper-consumer society that are open to criticism and which, deep down, account for a part of happiness but which also cause a great deal of unhappiness (solitude, psychological vulnerability, erratic behaviour, obesity, depression, anxiety, addiction). The hyper-consumer society is heavily criticised because there is excess criticism, excess credit, shopping, television, advertising, meat, fat, sugar etc. It is precisely this excess that should be criticised and not consumption itself, which actually provides people with a certain number of benefits. It is the logic of consumption that is negative. By this, I understand a dynamic that pushes us towards *living for consumption*. When consumption becomes our entire life, we are caught up in a vicious circle. Consumption should be a means and not an end in our lives. This perspective is not good, as human beings are not only consumers, we are also beings who think, who learn, who progress and who exceed ourselves. One should have a higher ideal of humankind than one that sets as its goals the consumption of brands and the eternal changing of products. I am not demonising consumption but when it becomes one's goal in life, the centre of one's life, one has come to a dead end, the wrong way forward.

But how can one reduce one's passions for consumption? My conviction is that we will not curb the influence of consumption with moral speeches of the type, 'it is evil, it is alienation; we should adopt a more frugal lifestyle and engage in de-consumption and de-growth'. I think that this type of criticism will in no way contribute to changing our world. Neither will more culturally focused television nor less advertising change the fundamental problem. We really have to understand that one can only reduce a passion for consumption by counter-attacking with other passions: as Spinoza said, we have to fight against one passion with another passion. It is not the pure reason of humankind that will curb the influence of consumption. We should invent what I call a pedagogy and a policy of passions. The goals that we should set ourselves should be goals for individuals, tasks capable of mobilising their affections, their passions, elsewhere than in the universe of consumption. And it is perhaps here that school can nowadays find its most noble mission to change the course of our times.

Who or what can convince people not to look for happiness in brands and commodities? I think that it is other passions, other desires, other interests, such as work, creativity, public engagement, art. What is important is to give human beings the ability to live for something else besides brands and the permanent turnover of products. We need not only ecological policies to preserve the environment but also what I call an ecology of mind, an ecology of our whole existence; I mean, no more than a greater equilibrium. Consumption is fine, as long as it is not excessive, and even then, we need other things in life. But if people do not have the essential tools to invest in these interests, nothing will stop the frenzy, the bulimia of consumption.

Criticism of hyper-consumption is useful and even necessary, in particular given the problems of the environment and ecological threats. This criticism should be repeated time and time again and you are engaged in this at this congress. But there is still something else which is fundamental, and that is to invent new forms of education and work that allow people to find individual identity and satisfaction outside the transient paradise of consumption. What is important is that, via other passions, humanity can put the consumer universe into perspective and in this way the acquisition of goods and brands would no longer be the focus and the ultimate goal of our existence.

Translated by Michael Dornan

Europe, the USA and China after the Crisis: Towards New Growth Models for Sustainability?

ALLAN LARSSON

I propose to address the fundamental question about the growth models of China, the USA and Europe – which is: will the financial crisis mark the end of the old, unsustainable models? Will there be new models, with a new balance between economic, social and environmental goals and policies? Or will China, the USA and Europe return to 'business as usual' as soon as our economies are recovering? Like David King, I will also take an optimistic view; however, one mixed with some scepticism.

I am engaged in a European think tank project on 'A new global order?' – question mark. It is an ambitious project, with the aim of understanding how the USA and China will find a way out of three traps:

- the debt trap, in which the USA is caught;

- the dollar trap, in which China is caught;

- and the climate trap, the dependency on fossil fuel, a trap in which China and the USA are caught – together with Europe and the rest of the world.

The purpose is also to find out how Europe can play a role in the emerging new global order of interdependence between the USA and China, and how Europe will rethink its own growth model – keeping in mind what Sir David King said about the successes of the twentieth century in bringing about health, longer life expectancy and prosperity.

We are still in the middle of the financial and economic crisis and it is still too early to start drawing or presenting any conclusions. What I shall do is:

- first, give my views on why the world is in this global mess;

- secondly, present three scenarios for the future, as a background to my last point;

- which is to discuss what governments are doing, and to make an assessment of the opportunities for a more sustainable order and the risks of a return to 'business as usual'.

If you wish to have a very brief summary of the origin of the crisis I would offer a three-word summary: *need, greed and feed* – poor people's need for housing, rich people's greed for money on Wall Street and elsewhere and the feeding of the US economy with cheap money, mainly from China and the rest of Asia.

The USA and China have played the leading roles in the build-up of the financial crisis. They are responsible for the major part of the global imbalances – the imbalance between savings and investment, with deficits in the USA and surpluses in China, an imbalance built up over the last five to ten years.

The nature of these imbalances has been summarised by Martin Wolf in the *Financial Times* in one expressive sentence: 'Capital now flows upstream, from the world's poor to the richest country of all.' Keep this sentence in mind as it will explain a lot of what has happened and why we have to change the growth models. 'Capital now flows upstream, from the world's poor to the richest country of all' – from hard-working, poor people in China and other countries in Southeast Asia to the richest country in the world, the USA; he could have added that some of the money is ending up in the pockets of the richest among the wealthy.

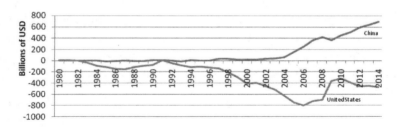

China and US Current Account Balances 1980–2014
(Source: IMF, *World Economic Outlook*, October 2009)

In the diagram above you can see this flow of capital expressed by IMF statistics. Below the zero line is the US current account deficit, a more or less permanent situation over many years. Above the zero line is the Chinese current account surplus, a phenomenon of the last five to seven years.

How did it happen? Here is the story. On the US side, there were some serious mistakes, three short-sighted policies, which led to the situation.

First, there was the deregulation of financial markets, which allowed banks to take huge risks. Secondly, this deregulation strategy was combined with – and supported by – two other policies, the Greenspan/Federal Reserve decision to lower interest rates in 2003, when the US economy was already in a strong recovery: 'subsidising borrowing in a booming economy', to quote Professor Michael Boskin at Stanford. Thirdly, on the top of that, President Bush made tax cuts to stimulate consumption further, and increased public expenditure.

This mix of deregulation, fiscal stimulus and monetary stimulus gave birth to the 'shadow banking system', which generated the consumption and housing boom. It was in this world that 'the subprime mortgage bubble blossomed and burst in the space of just six years, creating a crisis that made the Asian crisis, the dotcom crash and Enron look just like what they were: tremors and warning signals before the "extinction level event" of 2008', to quote the BBC financial reporter Paul Mason in his book, *Meltdown: The End of the Age of Greed.*[1]

However, the USA's 'borrow and spend' strategy would not have worked without someone having the opposite strategy, a 'save and lend' strategy. China became the perfect partner in this tango.

China had deregulated its foreign trade, invited the western world to invest in China and offered a deal: you bring investment and new technologies to us and we will offer you cheap labour. This 'inviting in' strategy was combined with an extreme neoliberal social policy, scrapping the old safety nets and letting individuals and families take all the risks.

This strategy made China the factory of the world, with booming exports. Chinese workers had to save money to compensate for the lack of social safety nets. Chinese state-owned enterprises could save their profits; the government did not ask for any dividends. A growing surplus in trade and current accounts was built up.

China saved and invested; the USA consumed and borrowed. This is how the USA and China became so dependent on each other.

China now has more than 2,200 billion dollars in foreign reserves, 60 per cent of which are in dollar assets. If the value of the Chinese currency goes up, as it should, or if the US dollar goes down, China will make a loss. Therefore, China has linked its currency to the dollar and will continue to support the USA – with its political blessing of the US economic policy and with promises to buy more US bonds. That is what I call 'the dollar trap' for China and 'the debt trap' for the USA.

On top of that, they are both in the climate trap. Their economic strategies have been based on energy from oil and coal: the USA and China are the major users of fossil fuel, responsible for almost half of global CO_2 emissions. They will continue on this path for many years. These growth strategies were not sustainable, neither financially, socially nor ecologically. The essence of the present crisis is that it is a crisis for these growth models.

Now, the big question: will the crisis lead to new models? The world will need a new global order; still we do not know whether this will happen or not.

Over the last year central banks, governments and parliaments have had to focus both on the immediate effects of the crisis and on long-term developments. They have been forced to address, simultaneously, four tasks, each of them extremely difficult:

- rescuing the financial system and bringing about a lasting recovery;

- reforming financial market regulations to avoid a new, deeper crisis;

- rebalancing the financial flows between Asia and the USA;

- and, finally, restructuring global energy systems for long-term sustainability.

One year after the collapse of Lehman Brothers, the symbol of the crisis, we can begin examining where all these actions will lead.

Let us look at three scenarios for the world after the crisis and compare these scenarios with what we know or what we can expect from the recovery strategies.

Scenario 1: 'Business as usual'?
The first one is a return to 'business as usual' and it is a pessimistic scenario. It is based on a quick recovery in the stock market, which we have seen, followed by a recovery in the economy, which is on its way. When growth is back again, the political support for reform will disappear and the changes in financial regulation will be marginal. Risk taking returns – as well as the bonus culture. The global imbalances between Asia and the USA will remain. The next crisis is just around the corner.

Scenario 2: The end of globalisation as we know it?
The second scenario is even more pessimistic. It is based on what many regard as a serious threat, a W-shaped recovery, which means that the present recovery in stock markets and the green

shoots in the economy will be interrupted by a new downturn, a financial and economic crisis, which will be very difficult to manage. This situation will lead to protectionism, trade conflicts, new accusations against China of an undervalued currency, and so on. On top of that the employment situation will worsen in all parts of the world.

Scenario 3: A new order – inside the USA and China, and between them?

The third scenario is an optimistic one, but perhaps not a realistic one. It is based on expectations that both China and the USA will implement new economic and social strategies and that these policies will work and will continue not only over the 2010 US Congress elections, but over the next ten years – including a breakthrough for a new global climate order.

Well, these are three possible scenarios, which are more or less realistic. There are developments that can be taken as evidence, positive and negative, of any of these three scenarios. Now, let us take a systematic view of these political, financial, social and environmental developments.

First, global politics. There is a clear sign of a fundamental change in this area. The old G8, consisting of the rich developed countries, has finally been replaced by the G20, including China, India, Brazil, Indonesia, South Africa and others. That is a big step forward in global governance.

Within the G20 China and the USA have taken the lead, in terms of recovery and in terms of reorientation of the policies of the past. President Obama has declared that 'the relations between the USA and China will shape the twenty-first century'. One leading US scholar on China has expressed the new political order in this way: 'No major global issue can be solved without China and the US, no major global issue can be solved by China and the US alone.'[2] Thus, in the political field there is the beginning of a new global order, a G2 world where China and the USA will do business together. In Europe we have to find out what this will mean and we will have to find new ways to protect our own interests.

Anyhow, it is quite clear that in this area the world has moved from business as usual into quite new territories.

Now, let us move to economic policy, and we can register some strong commitments both from China and the USA to a reorientation. Larry Summers, chief of President Obama's economic advisors, has summarised the new strategy in four points. The US economy will be:

- more export oriented, less consumption oriented;

- more environmentally oriented, less energy-production oriented;

- more bio- and software- and civil-engineering oriented and less financial-engineering oriented;

- more middle-class oriented, less oriented to income growth that is disproportionate in favour of a very small share of the population.

He does not stop there – he also demands others to reorient their economic strategies: 'if the US is going to be less the consumer of last resort, then other countries are going to need to be in different positions as well ...'

Well, what is China doing? China already took a decision in 2007 to seek a new growth strategy. The new goal was 'a harmonious society', a concept that has many meanings. It was triggered by internal criticism, opposition, strikes and even violent conflicts. The main policy implication is that social and environmental interests should play a bigger role in the Chinese development strategy. The economic crisis is a test case for this new strategy.

The financial and economic crisis hit China hard when global trade collapsed last autumn. China launched a bigger stimulus package than any other big global player. The new direction in Chinese economic policy, as it is expressed in the recovery plan, can be summarised in the following points:

- stimulus of internal demand to compensate for the collapse in external demand;

- stimulus of both consumption and investment (infrastructure, housing, energy);

- more focus on technology and innovation – to attract enterprises from abroad;

- more focus on China's 'going out' strategy – buying oil reserves, real estate, enterprises – instead of putting all the money in dollar assets.

There is a green element in this recovery but it is not quite clear how far-reaching it is. Experts have explained that a third of the resources will be used for environmentally friendly policies. There is also a recognition that the impact of the financial crisis has been significant: the crisis has eased the demand for energy and China has accelerated the implementation of its energy policy and the reform pace of energy management systems.

The stimulus package is one thing. A more fundamental question is how China and the USA will play their cards in the negotiations in the run-up to Copenhagen in December 2009. Will President Obama and his Chinese host strike a deal when they meet in Beijing in the middle of November? This is a great opportunity – let us wait and see.

Now, let us look at the social dimension. It is obvious that China's extremely neoliberal social policies are a severe problem, not only for unprotected people, but also for China as a country and for the rest of the world. Both the World Bank and the IMF are pushing China to build up a better, decent, social protection system.

Yes, there are some steps in the right direction. They are part of the 'harmonious society' strategy and some of these policies – on health, education, income – have been strengthened in the recovery plan. But there is still a long, long way to go.

What is the role of Europe in this emerging new global order? First of all, we can say, as European leaders used to say, that the financial crisis did not originate in Europe. We can add that Europe played a key role in rescuing the financial system last autumn and that the euro has proved its stability and strength. We can also remind ourselves that Europe started a recovery before the USA. Our social model is more advanced and robust and a stabilising factor. Last but not least, Europe has taken the lead in the climate negotiations by offering a more ambitious deal than any of the other big players.

However, Europe will need to realise the fact that China and the USA will take the global political leadership: 'No major global issue can be solved without China and the US, no major global issue can be solved by China and the US alone.' Europe has to come up with a convincing answer to this new global order to be able to protect its own interest in many fields.

The next few years will be difficult and crucial for the European social model. Fiscal discipline will certainly be needed, but also initiatives to develop a new European growth model. We can do better.

We can do better on science, technology and innovation. The USA and China are giving priority to investment in these fields. Europe is lagging behind. A new start for the knowledge-based economy should be a top priority.

We can do better on the social dimension. People will need security in change, and social protection has to play a fundamental role in the transformation of our societies; to do so, we have to make social policy a productive factor.

We have to deliver on our commitments to energy, environment and climate. Europe has to prepare for the post-Copenhagen process and make the transformation of our old unsustainable energy system a driving force for a new period of innovation, investment and employment. Will this lead to new growth models, to a new sustainable global order?

Let me end by returning to the three scenarios I introduced at the beginning. Will we return to 'business as usual'? Will we see a W-shaped recovery with great risks that it will lead to the 'end of globalisation as we know it'? Or will we enter into a new global order? Today, nobody knows. The risks of a return to business as usual are great. However, a crisis is an opportunity – if well-managed.

I leave it to you to think it through. Next year, when the

Gulbenkian Foundation has its October conference, it will be time to draw some conclusions about the most dramatic years in our time.

Notes

1 Paul Mason, *Meltdown: The End of the Age of Greed* (London: Verso, 2009).
2 Thomas Fingar of Stanford University, in interview, October 2009.

Citizen Action on Climate Change and Sustainable Development

MALINI MEHRA

This is going to be a real change in pace, and a change in focus also. I'm not going to stand here and talk to you about philosophical discussions or academic investigations into climate change. I'm going to talk about action. Action that has been taking place around the world, most recently just last Saturday 24 October. I'm going to finish with some news about that, but what I would like to do today is to provide you with an outline of climate activism around the world today.

I was asked to speak on the subject of citizens as actors in sustainable development and what I would like to focus on is climate change activism. I will address the development of campaigning on climate change in recent years and months, with a particular focus on the negotiations taking place in December in Copenhagen, the Conference of the Parties 15 (COP15).

I shall begin by outlining some of the main organisational forms that climate change activism has taken over the course of the last 20 years. The first organisation that I'm going to talk about is the Climate Action Network (CAN), followed by the Global Campaign for Climate Action (GCCA). A few of you, I think, will be familiar with the GCCA, which is the most recent incarnation of global climate activism. Next I shall discuss a few very specific campaigns such as Tck Tck Tck, Seal the Deal, and 350.org. Then I'm going to talk about some of the Global Days of Action, two of which have occurred already this year. I will focus on the second of these, the one that occurred on 24 October. And finally, I'm going to reflect on some of the things that have been achieved; what have the results been, and what does this kind of activism, this kind of campaigning, tell us about the future of this kind of citizen engagement?

I begin with the Climate Action Network. About 20 years ago, when I became active in climate campaigns, we were working largely through our international organisations and our national organisations. About 20 years ago, I was with the largest global federation of autonomous national environmental organisations, Friends of the Earth International. We had an active group in Portugal.

Around that time, some time after Rio, it was decided that what was really needed was some kind of a platform that brought together organisations and networks like ours. This became the Climate Action Network.

It started as a platform for European and North American (primarily USA-based) environmental organisations. But since that time it has grown into a globally representative network. It's a well-organised community of individuals and organisations, primarily – not just campaigning organisations, but many which have a research or academic or policy focus. CAN brings together a mixed tribe of organisations from around the world who historically have worked very, very well together. They've had a very clear focus on climate change as a major problem to be solved.

In recent years that relationship has become a little strained, as organisations have entered into the mix that do not come from an environmental background, such as trade unions, development organisations, and so on, and they have brought different emphases. So, although diversity, that kind of multiculturalism, in a global climate community is to be welcomed, it has created tensions in terms of the forms and political strategies to be followed.

CAN International now has regional offices. My organisation, for example, is a member of CANSA (CAN South Asia), the regional climate network that brings together the countries in our region.

One of the benefits of CAN if you're a member, however, is that it offers a unique source of information – on what's happening around the world on climate change, via the CAN-Talk list-serve. This is a fabulous source of information, comment and insight – and it's unstoppable. Virtually every five minutes someone somewhere around the world will post a message to the CAN-Talk list-serve with the latest press release, or the latest report on the latest catastrophe or controversy that has come out.

You can spend your whole life following CAN-Talk and it will make you into a supremely well-informed campaigner. So we use that. As an organisation based in India, we find we are often way ahead of the mainstream press or our policymakers because we have access to information through sources such as the CAN network and CAN-Talk.

As in the wider world, networks such as CAN are challenged by differences of political opinion, approach and strategy. CAN is still to a large extent dominated by the same polarised 'North–South' form of thinking present in the climate negotiations, where – roughly put – the North (developed world) is bad and the South (developing world) is good. This North–South divide has been a permanent fissure in terms of interpretation of the political context of climate policy within CAN – and it creates problems for people such as me, who do not share this world view.

About two-and-a-half years ago, something different was started by a few people connected with CAN and a group of outsiders such as ourselves. This body finally emerged at the beginning of 2009 and was called the Global Campaign for Climate Action. It brought together organisations from around the world and this was beyond the CAN international community. GCCA reached out beyond NGOs to the trade unions, to the International Trade Unions Congress, to a whole variety of faith groups and they became really active on climate change. Some of you may recall that the World Council of Churches as far back as 2002 in

Johannesburg, and again in 2005 and 2007, started making pronouncements on climate change. It was the first organised religious group to begin doing that. Now we find many, many different faith groups who have become involved and active on this issue.

The GCCA has now swelled to become a vibrant and active force for climate action, bringing a variety of stakeholders together on one common platform calling for a Fair, Ambitious and Binding deal – a FAB deal – to come out of Copenhagen. It has found traction around the world and we now have, for example, more than 2 million people worldwide who have signed a petition calling for a FAB deal. The GCCA has also developed a special intelligence and strategy development body, which guides action – the Nervecentre, a very useful body bringing together strategic analysis and providing recommendations to the wider GCCA grouping for action. I contribute to this from India.

One of the things that has emerged in recent months is the need to increase visibility of some of the most affected and vulnerable countries on the planet in terms of climate change. A number of these vulnerable countries had come together originally in a political group called AOSIS, the Alliance of Small Island States. This was small and relatively inconsequential at the time of Kyoto in 1997, even though it had some very powerful leaders, such as Ambassador Slade from Samoa, who spoke forcefully about the need for climate change policy making to be attentive to the unique disadvantages faced by small Pacific Island nations such as his.

In the last year, however, AOSIS has re-emerged. It has come from virtually nowhere to be a powerful moral force on the climate issue. Not as powerful and influential as many of us would wish it to be – certainly not within the G-77/China political grouping within the United Nations. But AOSIS has resurfaced and has resurfaced largely as a result of new vision and new blood. New people have joined, such as Ambassador Dessima Williams from Grenada, the permanent representative of Grenada in the Caribbean to the UN; and President Nasheed, the 42-year-old president of the Maldives, who was elected at the beginning of the year after 30 years of dictatorship in this small island nation, the lowest island nation in the world. Incidentally, President Nasheed has done a number of amazing things to bring the plight of his island and the issues it faces to public attention. For example, just last week, he launched the 350.org campaign. He and his entire Cabinet of ten other Cabinet ministers held the world's first underwater Cabinet meeting. After half-an-hour of the underwater meeting, they signed a petition to global leaders calling for action on climate change.

So, he's been involved in very media-savvy publicity events – stunts, some people would say, but defining campaigns. Individuals such as Nasheed and Decima, and a few others from AOSIS, have tried to put AOSIS on the map now, to ensure that the high moral ground AOSIS can occupy can translate into real impact in terms of changing North–South dynamics and the terms of the policy debates in climate negotiations.

The other interesting thing that has been happening among the climate vulnerable countries, and that many of us in the climate campaigning world have been supporting, is that we see the least developed countries – (around 80 to 90 per cent of the countries of the world) coming together and joining hands with AOSIS.

A really interesting thing happened in Bonn in June 2009, at the preparatory meeting of the United Nations Framework Convention on Climate Change (UNFCCC) for the negotiations at Copenhagen. This was the third meeting in Bonn of the climate negotiations, just before Bangkok in September 2010. (The final preparatory meeting of the UNFCCC for Copenhagen is in Barcelona in November 2010.) There was a coming together of AOSIS and the Least Developed Countries (LDCs) around a common platform, and that common platform was that 'we are the most vulnerable and we need to shout it from the rooftops and make sure that our concerns are heard before those of the countries that have historically defined the agenda within the G77 and the major powers'. In a sense it was a slap in the face for the traditional G77 and G20 blocs, but also for OPEC and the oil lobby, which has virtually taken over the G77 in terms of the climate change and energy agenda. So, these are some very interesting political developments and our role as campaigners is to engage with them and reflect the urgency of the science to bring to the fore a better-quality political discussion with greater impact.

A recent development in the GCCA, beginning in early 2009, was the idea of having a global campaign that resonated with people and would drive attention to and ambitions for Copenhagen.

We adopted the slogan 'Tck Tck Tck', which sounds like the ticking of a clock, as the logo for the movement, to signify the countdown to COP15. This is going to be our identity now for the rest of the year.

Tck Tck Tck has attracted a huge number of followers from around the world; people from Desmond Tutu to Bono, celebrities and non-celebrities around the world are supporting this movement. They've started to conduct all sorts of actions, whether it's something straightforward such as planting a tree, or converting a company to be an icon for a low-carbon future. These are examples that have actually taken place in the name of Tck Tck Tck, so Tck Tck Tck is now a big player.

The other thing that has happened, which is very interesting because it is unprecedented, is the Seal the Deal campaign. This is a UN-led campaign, and this is the first time in the history of the UN that the body as a whole has decided to become an NGO, so to speak. One of the things that this means is that every major UN document published now starts with the Seal the Deal logo stamped on it, to remind readers and delegates of the need to reach agreement at Copenhagen. The fact that the UN leadership has managed to agree on this, given the differences between many of the agencies within the UN, in itself is quite an achievement, I think.

So, the UN has been leading this and we've worked very closely with them to push the Seal the Deal campaign. The Secretary-General of the United Nations, Ban Ki-moon, has been a fantastic ally. He's clearly thinking of his legacy beyond his term and wishes to be seen as a pivotal figure in getting the world to acknowledge climate change, which in his words is 'the defining challenge of our age'. The Seal the Deal campaign is one of the UN's manifestations of engagement on the issue.

To return briefly to the GCCA. I'd like to share with you another of the things that we've done as GCCA. One of the world's first Global Days of Action on climate change occurred on 21 September at the UN, because that was the week that began the UN Climate Change Summit, which coincided with the General Assembly meeting at the UN in New York. At the time, Tck Tck Tck placed a newspaper advertisement in the *Financial Times* and the *International Herald Tribune* to impress upon world leaders the importance of using the financial crisis as an important moment to redouble our efforts towards a greener, low-carbon, more competitive economy, based on a different business model.

What I want to finish with now is to tell you a little about 350.org. 350.org is a movement started by Bill McKibben. Bill is a journalist and has written for papers such as the *New York Times* for over 30 years. He was one of the first people to write about climate change. For example, he covered Jim Hansen's testimony before the US Senate in the 1970s. He's a pretty shy, retiring kind of guy; however, Bill had this genius idea which was, let's just focus on 350 as a kind of magic number.

Now, for a long time, we climate campaigners have been focusing on the number 450 parts per million. That is, 450 ppm of CO_2 equivalent gases in the atmosphere. In Kyoto we were arguing among ourselves, should we push for 450 or should we agree to 550, because it was 550 ppm that was set as the so-called 'safe' level by governments and climate science hadn't pushed as far ahead as it has now. What we have found out since is that 550 ppm is by no means safe, and neither is 450 ppm.

What increasing numbers of scientists are telling us now – and it's interesting that in recent weeks we've had people such as Rajendra Pacahuri, the chair of the IPCC (Intergovernmental Panel on Climate Change) coming out backing this – is that 350 ppm is the only possible safe level of atmospheric carbon dioxide concentration that we should be aiming for.

This is what is happening now. But back when Bill started, there wasn't such a degree of scientific consensus. There were mavericks and outliers; people like Jim Hansen who would say, '350 parts per million, is it! We've got to focus on that.' So Bill went out on a wing and a prayer and started going around the world and talking to people – evangelising basically. I remember last year in Sweden at the Tallberg Forum there was great support for the idea of backing the 350 ppm campaign.

The success lay in the simplicity of the 'ask', or the call to action, which was:

> Look, we are in peril as a civilisation and one way that I want to get that across to you is by helping you understand the science. The science tells us that we have to reduce our emissions – which are currently at 387 almost 390 ppm, up from pre-industrial times when they were 287 ppm – reduce them down to a safe level. This safe level is 350 ppm. If we don't take steps to ensure this, if we continue with business-as-usual, then by 2100 we could see global CO_2 concentrations at 600 ppm – which roughly correlates to about 5 or 6°C of warming. This basically means that that's the end of a comfortable stable environment for life to exist and civilisation to flourish.

This was the core of the message and its simplicity worked. The penny started to drop everywhere. I remember a discussion about 350 in India at the beginning of last year. An American activist came to talk to us about 350.org and asked for help. I said, 'Sure, we'll help', because we help anyone who wants to work on climate change, but then I found that within a matter of a few months this movement was spreading like wildfire. And it spread like wildfire for two reasons, I think. The first was the simplicity of the message and the simplicity of the 'ask'. It's a very low threshold to engage people at, disarmingly simple. Bill was saying, and his acolytes around the world were saying, 'Look, all you have to do to join forces and express your concern about climate change, all you need to do is something visual, graphic, interesting with this number, 350, that's it. We'll help show it around the world and spread the message that the global target for carbon concentration in the atmosphere should not exceed 350 ppm.' You couldn't have a lower threshold, a lower entry point to a campaign than that. The second thing that he did was that he threw himself into working with young people. Now young people around the world are *the* transformational force; they are the ones who have given the climate change issue the impact it has had – not necessarily in political terms, but in terms of cultural energy.

So, Bill has now worked with young people who are coming to the fore. Our offices are often packed with young people, who are coming to us to say: 'We want to work with you, we want to do this, want to do that.' I just got an email from my office two days ago in Bangalore, saying: 'Malini, these young people are crazy, they want to do everything!'

This is wonderful, because it just shows that we've really tapped into something here. This is about the future and these young people are the link to it. The other key to understanding the growth and power of the 350.org movement is its use of communications technology as a result of tapping into the youth vibe. This is what has made this work.

Bill's people went around the world. They *really* went around the world. They went to Tuvalu, they went to Tanzania, they went to Beijing, they came to India – several times – they set up base camp in Nepal, and what they did was, they grabbed the young people and they said: 'We are going to use the media that you understand, so, everything from Flickr and SMSing to Twitter, we will give you little Flip cameras', tiny video cameras you can record interviews on. Then they set up mobile media training camps and communications camps for young people, such that by the time 24 October came around – the Global Day of Action – we knew something big was going to happen.

And something big did happen. That day, Google called it 'the biggest story the world has ever seen'. They said so because on that day there were 5,284 organised rallies taking place, on every continent and in most countries and regions of the planet. This was the first time that such a coordinated campaign had taken place literally around the world. As for the numbers, we know how many events took place because the 350.org Web site made it easy to keep track. The Web site made it easy to communicate: 'If you're doing something, you're organising a march or you're just going up to a mountain, whatever it is, if you're showing an image of 350 ppm, put it up on the Web site and let the world see.'

So, that's how we know that these legitimate campaigns or rallies or actions actually took place in 181 countries around the world. And think of it, there are 192 nations engaged in the Copenhagen climate negotiations and virtually all of them have been touched by citizens in their countries who are calling for action.

Perhaps parts per million of CO_2 sounds too obscure an idea to attract crowds on six continents, but there were thousands of people in the streets, from Togo and Ethiopia and Paraguay to Seattle and London and Sydney. For campaigners like me, this stuff is gold dust, because we sweat our guts out to get people engaged on this, and what they managed to do with 350.org was to use this very simple and elegant scientific concept to amazing effect.

I'm sure we're going to hear some objections to 350, but the fact is that it has touched people at a very visible level and made them understand in a way that very few of our earlier campaigns have managed. It's certainly not the kind of bureaucratic and policy-driven form of campaigning that we did at CAN, in the happy bubble of climate change negotiations. But we're now getting the kind of media attention that we never thought possible.

Incidentally, it's well worth taking a look at the slideshow on the 350.org Web site to get a sense of some of the things that took place around the world. You'll see schoolchildren and housewives and every single segment of society in some way represented in some of these pictures, and these are just a few from almost 19,000 that have been submitted so far. So there's plenty to see!

I want to end with a couple of questions for you, to do with the effectiveness of this kind of campaign. As someone who is involved in the organisation and promotion of these kinds of campaigns, I also deal every day with the negotiations and the policy world, and I find that although these campaigns are helping to change public perceptions, they are not impacting on the politics and trade-offs that we see in daily negotiations.

The heads of the negotiations and the chief negotiators, even the head of the UNFCCC in Bonn, are very welcoming of this kind of activity, because they want the public engaged. But it's not really changing the political process. The question is, how can these kinds of campaigns help engage with the politics and change the current state of climate politics?

Let's look at the USA, for example. Yes, we love to trash the USA, because at the Federal Government level they've been in the dark ages for the last decade – but it's a different story around the country. If you look at the 350.org campaigns, you'll see that the largest number of them were held in the USA.

Is it that maybe the next step for us is to gather together people who have done the minimum thing – which is to come up with a nice little picture or a nice visual using the number 350 – to go out there and engage in the political process? Because it seems to be only when politicians fear that there's actually going to be a cost politically that they'll start to be serious about making the kind of deals that we need to see happen in Copenhagen.

Emissions Trading Schemes and the Future of the Carbon Economy

PEDRO MARTINS BARATA

My theme is not the most interesting, or rather, it is one of the most interesting to me, but it is difficult to transmit the enthusiasm I feel for the issue in the fascinating way that Malini did.

Malini spoke of 'a happy bubble of climate change negotiations'. I have lived in that bubble for ten years now as a climate negotiator for the Portuguese Government and have followed the implementation of the Kyoto Protocol; and now with responsibilities at European level, I am still following the post-Kyoto negotiations, which it is hoped will end in Copenhagen.

First of all, what is at stake in Copenhagen? In technical terms, what is going to be done in Copenhagen?

Two years ago in Bali, while Portugal held the presidency of the European Union, an action plan was negotiated at the thirteenth United Nations Framework Climate Change Conference, which would lead, two years later, to the conclusion of a new agreement on climate change in Copenhagen. Why the need for this new agreement and why now? Because the Kyoto Protocol establishes a deadline to achieve stipulated targets; that deadline ends in 2012. There are no emissions limits negotiated beyond 2012. Soon, it will be necessary to carry out new negotiations about the new post-2012 emissions limit. More importantly, the elephant that left the room some years ago has since returned and it needs to be accommodated and a bigger room needs to be created for it. We are talking about the USA. The USA has returned; and has returned in a way and with a force that some suspected but few were fully aware of. Today, using the words of Allan Larsson, climate negotiation is increasingly a bilateral negotiation between China and the USA, with the European Union playing a role that is not entirely secondary, but one that is not as crucial as it was when the Kyoto Protocol was forged. We can say, somewhat light-heartedly, that when the Kyoto Protocol was negotiated it was between the interests and vision of Europe and the USA, with a final proposal presented to the rest of the world. This time will be different. It will be different because China has a new role, as do India and Brazil. It won't be the same because, let us hope, the results of this new alliance between the AOSIS group (Alliance of Small Island States) and less developed countries will provide them with a more active role in the negotiations. In short, what is at stake is the conclusion of the Bali Action Plan: A New Architecture for a Climate Regime. A crucial point of that new architecture (and one where I must confess to being profoundly disappointed with our European leaders) is the funding for action on mitigation (one year on, Europe still does not have a proposal on the table on how to fund the mitigation action necessary to achieve the proposed objective: 2°C above the pre-industrial average).

However, there are other factors involved in these negotiations: the distribution of intellectual property rights for new low carbon emissions technology. The critical debate here is with China, India and Brazil. How and in what form will we have a new system of specific intellectual property rights for low carbon emissions technology? In addition to this, there is an issue that I will focus on in the latter part of my contribution: at Copenhagen there is also the issue of the continuation and expansion of the carbon market as the main support mechanism for international carbon mitigation. Finally, and obviously, there is the reintegration of the USA into the international climate community.

To put it more simply and straightforwardly, we are looking at a simple negotiation about how to cut up the emissions pie. There are various formulae that have been presented at international level to say what this negotiation is all about. One simple formula: let's imagine a common asset, which is the world's atmosphere, and a right to use that common asset for a certain amount of time. That right is limited or has to be limited, i.e. there is an emissions pie that we have to share, both among ourselves and with the coming generations – and we have to understand which different criteria can be used to share that pie.

The starting point is to choose the target temperature. To some degree, this is a highly technocratic way of summing up what Malini so brilliantly revealed. Addressing the climate issue implies asking ourselves, at this moment, what world do we want a hundred years from now and what are the impacts we are prepared to live with. We already know that some impacts are inevitable. Why? Because the current emissions levels already put us on a path that locks us into such inevitable impacts. What we have to consider and determine collectively is the level and impacts that we consider acceptable for future generations. Putting aside ethical issues about the viability of one generation taking such decisions for another, how can we make that choice? We have some scenarios from the Intergovernmental Panel on Climate Change that can help us; these come from the Fourth Assessment Report published a few years ago. Since then, scientific consensus, as identified so ably by Malini, has portrayed these scenarios in a more negative light. Nevertheless, based on this assessment report, the majority of observers chose, in what could be considered a somewhat arbitrary choice, a 2°C rise as the threshold of what we desire as the new world climate balance at the end of 2100.

This choice is political, not scientific. The basic information is scientific but the choice is very political, and it is very political for one simple reason. With a threshold of 2°C, there are entire countries that will disappear from the map. So the objective that the leaders of the European Union, including our Prime Minister, committed themselves to is in fact a 'death sentence' for certain countries, the so-called small island states that Malini referred to and which are grouped together in the negotiating group known as the Alliance of Small Island States (AOSIS). To better illustrate this point, at the last meeting in Bangkok, badges were being given out by that group. They read: '1.5°C to stay alive' (or, 'one point five to stay alive').

This is the first moral dilemma that we have to deal with. Whatever the arguments, Europe chose 2°C. And at the moment, all climate negotiation for Copenhagen is focused on 2°C and a target concentration of 450 parts per million (ppm) CO_2 equivalent. Therefore, I would not say that the 350 ppm campaign is out of synch as such; it is possibly out of synch in terms of timing, in the sense that it has information that our leaders did not have two or three years ago – but the truth is, it is far from that which is the fundamental goal of the negotiations for the major players. Let us hope that AOSIS becomes a major player in Copenhagen.

Choosing a target concentration is also choosing the risk of not achieving it, which means, even choosing the objective of 450 ppm, which is the top part of the graph, means a fifty-fifty chance of not achieving 2°C. Or rather, even this objective of 450 ppm is a half-hearted objective and unsubstantiated by science. If someone negotiated a fire insurance policy, they would not want an insurance policy that only worked 50 per cent of the time. The Stern Review – the report commissioned by the British Government on the costs of climate change – published two years ago, stated that 'even this political objective that European leaders had defined was already practically off the map'.

The third step is choosing the trajectory and objectives of reduction and this step is fundamental. At the G20 meetings, some steps have been taken towards agreeing the final objective of 2°C and the objective of 450 ppm, but now we get to the lion's share of the problem, which is: choosing the emissions scenario and trajectories for the different countries and different negotiations groups. Obviously, all of us have an economic interest in others reducing and not us, and that is the nature of the negotiation – the so-called Prisoner's Dilemma.

Trajectories are everything in this negotiating game: for each level of long-term balance stabilisation (450, 350) there are various possible reduction trajectories. Once again, these trajectories may be scientifically derived but choosing them is eminently political, because the choice determines who reduces and who bears the reduction costs. The European Union advocates an objective for developed countries of a reduction of 25 to 40 per cent. This figure is not a magic number; it is a number that comes from the IPCC – however, choosing it implies a challenge to developing countries and to the rapidly growing economies in particular. For an endpoint of 2°C to be achieved, with us developed countries aiming for between 25 and 40 per cent, other developing nations have to have autonomous reductions of between 15 and 30 per cent in terms of their long-term trajectory. It implies a particular way of sharing the emissions pie. It is here that the negotiations at Copenhagen become key, in terms of mitigation.

What does this have to do with the carbon market? The carbon market, historically speaking (over the last five years), has served to reduce the cost of meeting the previously fixed standards, therefore helping us find more efficient solutions. It has also served (or so the argument goes) to make the more developed countries more ambitious, knowing that the cost of achieving the proposed goals is lower. It is this that is reflected in the European Union energy and climate package. The European Union unilaterally proposes the achievement of a 20% reduction by 2020, rising to 30%, thus within the 25% to 40% category, if there is an agreement at Copenhagen; however, the increase from 20% to 30% is, in part, because there will be a degree of flexibility provided by the carbon market.

There is one very important caveat here. The carbon market can only work if there is a quantified reduction goal. A criticism of the carbon market is that, to a certain point, it dilutes objectives. In some cases and mechanisms of the carbon market, this is true. However, the theory and the practice demonstrate that the carbon market is no substitute for a quantified goal and, above all, it is no substitute for the active role of the state. The carbon market is, after all, just a regulation formula and needs a clear institutional framework to include:

- *Ambitious quantified goals.* When goals are not ambitious, we know what happens, because that is what happened in 2006 in the European Union. When the member states had a degree of autonomy in establishing goals for their industries, they used it, abused it, conceded emissions rights over and above what was necessary, and the truth is that the carbon market collapsed and the price rapidly dropped to zero. Therefore, quantified goals have to be ambitious.

- *A far more ambitious emissions verification and report system* than the one normally used in environmental regulation. Because emissions have a price, it is absolutely necessary that those emissions are counted, quantified and verified, and in a credible fashion. This is an advantage that the European Union has over other countries on an international level; because we have had an active carbon market since 2005, we have an emissions reporting and verification system for half of our economies, in the most competitive sectors, which is more advanced than what we see in other countries, including developed countries.

- When all is said and done, the carbon market needs *a clear legal framework and punitive sanctions* for those not meeting their commitments. In Europe, each excess tonne of emissions costs 100 euros. It is prohibitive, to say the least. It is that sanction that guarantees compliance by our industries.

In the Copenhagen agreement, the carbon market can perform a third function. Given such reluctance to and, I would say, almost a moral quandary about demanding quantified reduction goals from certain countries, like China, India and Brazil, what is actually demanded is that those countries contribute to that important baseline deviation, with emissions reductions that are their own responsibility but that are not reflected in a quantified goal. So, what we are going to do is use an incentives mechanism, which is the carbon market itself. We have now arrived at the truly technocratic and bureaucratic part of my contribution. Let us consider an emissions trajectory that is business as usual, for example in the cement sector of China. What is on the table, which are pre-

Copenhagen negotiable documents, is that China has to make a commitment to present action plans, for example for the cement sector, that reduce its emissions in this sector. These should be contributions from individual countries. Over and above these contributions, there will be funded contributions, often from the public resources of developed countries, and let us hope that they are not counted as public aid to development (actually, that is the main theme of the Council of Europe). Then, after having reduced those emissions further via intergovernmental public funding, we will be able to arrive at a point where we can credit all of the reductions that China manages in its sector, funding them via the carbon market and transporting them on credit from the countries that funded them. This is the global concept behind much of the negotiated text in Copenhagen. Obviously, there is much to untangle both here and in the post-Copenhagen period, but the principles are now in the negotiated text and, as always, the focus of the negotiation is going to be the amount: the emissions ceilings, the emissions rights.

Between the NAMAs (nationally appropriate mitigation actions) that can be funded, there are issues like how to finance the emissions markets in China and India. It is said that China has not done anything. Currently, China has emissions market pilot schemes; it has renewable energy certificate system projects, which are, in some cases, more advanced and more ambitious than the European systems. India already has a renewable energy credit market.

In terms of the rest of the carbon market, a few years ago, here at the Gulbenkian, I made a presentation about possible carbon market configurations. One such configuration foresaw the establishment of mutiple regional emissions trading schemes. The prospects for the set-up of this carbon market are much simpler nowadays. Today we have the prospect of a single American market: after the introduction of a bill in the House of Representatives called the Waxman-Markey Bill, recently a new bill was introduced in the Senate by Senator John Kerry and Senator Barbara Boxer, which aims to create an American emissions trading market. This market is four times greater than the

European one and the reason for this is very simple: it encompasses 85 per cent of the sectors of North American emissions, while ours only covers 50 per cent. Again, the reason is very simple. The reduction effort required of these sectors is proportionately greater. And here we can dispel a myth: Europe likes to boast about its leadership on climate issues. If truth be told, depending on how you look at it, the North American goals on the table can be considered far more ambitious – they start from a higher level. The USA has done little or nothing in terms of reducing emissions in the last ten years and is now proposing to make up the ground that the European Union has covered in the last ten years in twenty. It is also interesting that the emissions market is expanding beyond typically developed countries, to countries like Mexico and South Korea.

In all of this, there is a major challenge and large black cloud hanging over Copenhagen with regard to the new American position. Currently, the American position is: we have an internal system that is much better than the majority of nation-states with reduction commitments. We have an environmental policy that is considerably more advanced that many of our partners, including Europe; we do not have to or want to be subject to an international emissions report system, which means we do not want to have a situation where in 2017, or 2018, a national inventory of North American emissions is reviewed by an international team of experts and is found not to conform. The idea of non-conformity on the part of the USA with an international obligation is not part of the current American position. The current justification is that such a subordination of the American emissions trading system to an international one is impossible within the political framework on today's Capitol Hill. This creates serious complications for the entire architecture that we Europeans, and others, had imagined for post-Kyoto. What did Kyoto essentially do? Apart from emissions trading and the clean development mechanism, which are interesting, at the heart of Kyoto was the creation of a quantified obligation of emissions limitation and reduction, reported at international level and verified annually. Every country that has quantified goals reports every year and is subject to independent verification and that verification has teeth, and it bites. For us to get an idea, Croatia, which is a recent ratifier of the Kyoto Protocol, has just seen its inventory turned down at international level. It is exactly this that the USA cannot conceive. They cannot conceive that the treatment that was given to Croatia in Bangkok two weeks ago could apply to their fulfilment of their international level. At the same time, the USA does not accept an accounting unit in terms of emissions at international level. They want less stringent international monitoring and verification rules. They neither want nor accept being subject to any sanction for non-fulfilment. The reason given is that it may not be ratified by Congress. When this position was increasingly taken in the lead-up to Bangkok, there was some unease. That unease was increased further when, at the beginning of Bangkok, the European Union said: 'Actually, we agree with certain aspects of the American position and we also don't want to create an international accounting unit and we also want a single international agreement that covers all situations, for developed countries and developing countries.'

The issue is that the price to pay to have the USA committed to emissions reductions at international level may mean doing away with the architecture of Kyoto. For those, like me, who have spent ten years in this happy bubble, this is rather distressing. Perhaps, this has to be the price. Kyoto will have to undergo a metamorphosis for us to have a 'global' agreement. Within its metamorphosis we only have one reasonable certainty, and that is that the carbon market is going to expand. If the Kerry-Boxer proposal is approved, and it has a strong chance of being approved after certain recent events, the market will quadruple almost instantly and, in the long term, developing countries will create emissions trading schemes similar to those of developed countries. We have the cases that I have already mentioned of China, India, Brazil, Mexico and South Korea. All of them have, in some way or another, carbon market pilot schemes. Whether those pilot schemes will be in the Copenhagen agreement, it is difficult to say at the moment, but we will see what Copenhagen has to offer us.

Translated by Daniel Boyce

Charting a Course for the Future of the Oceans: Present State and Future Perspectives

JULIE PACKARD

The last quarter century has brought with it unprecedented changes in our environment, but only recently have we extended our attention to the largest living space on Earth – the oceans. The issues facing our seas range from pollution and coastal habitat loss to invasive species and overfishing. An emerging threat that over-arches all others is the impact of global climate change. Motivating the public to solve these problems will be the great challenge of our generation, and we have a long way to go. While many people are concerned about the environment, few extend their knowl-edge or action to ocean issues. Still, there are hopeful signs of progress, including a growing consumer movement in favour of more sustainably caught seafood and a global push to create marine protected areas where marine life can survive and thrive.

Why care about the oceans? We live on a water planet. Our world is nearly three-quarters covered with ocean, and in terms of volume, over 90 per cent of the living space on Earth is in the sea. Our oceans drive world climate, produce most of the oxygen we breathe and provide primary protein for a billion people. Clearly, our lives depend on a future with healthy ocean ecosystems that can continue to provide these essential ecosystem services. Unfortunately, our growing human impact is taking a huge toll on the health of the ocean systems that we depend on for our very survival.

We once believed that the oceans were so vast, no human activity could possibly affect them. We now know that is not true. Today, ocean ecosystems nearly everywhere are in a state of decline. The causes are varied but can be summarised in a simple way: what we put in and what we take out. What we put in includes nitrogen from fertilisers and waste, metals and other toxins, invasive species and carbon. What we take out consists of habitat destruction from development, and importantly, the marine life we harvest for food and fodder.

Pollution was once thought to be the most pressing human impact on the sea, as the ocean has always been viewed as a convenient way to dispose of human waste products. With nearly 7 billion people, mostly living on the coast, this continues to be a huge issue. But there is a growing recognition of the problem with this approach and advances have been made in wastewater treatment such that in many areas today wastewater treatment has improved. Today, scientists believe that the biggest pollution threat to the oceans is diffuse pollution from farms and cities, especially from nitrogen fertilisers used in agriculture. Over 50 per cent of all the synthetic nitrogen fertiliser ever used has been used since 1985, and use is increasing as we strive to increase agricultural production to feed a growing population. As a result of run-off into coastal waters, we now see a growing number of ocean dead zones where nitrogen pollution has created low-oxygen areas where no marine life can survive.

The next major issue facing ocean health is coastal habitat loss. Three-quarters of us live on the coast. As a result, the majority of coastal wetlands have been filled or degraded to make way for cities, losing habitat areas that are essential nursery grounds for fisheries. These areas provide essential protection from storms, as demonstrated to us in a real way by the tremendous impact of the recent major tsunami and hurricane disasters.

An issue of growing concern is the impact of invasive species, as our global society enables people and products to easily travel from place to place, often carrying unwelcome species. Vast numbers of non-native marine species have been introduced to bays and coastal systems through ship ballast water, disrupting native species and causing negative consequences for humans. While laws have been created to stem this tide, the problem is far from over. As an example, San Francisco Bay hosts over 175 species of introduced marine invertebrates, fish, algae and higher plants.

Of all the human activities conducted in the ocean, perhaps the one with the most visibility and immediate concern is the impact of fishing. Fishing has been part of the human enterprise for millennia, but only in the past 50 years have we reached the point where our extraction of marine life is beyond the point of sustainability. The state of today's global fisheries is dire. Scientists predict that today 90 per cent of the large top predator fish – high-value fish like tuna, shark and swordfish – are gone. The way we fish today is highly wasteful, with 25 per cent of our harvest consisting of wasted catch of non-targeted species. Thousands of trawlers ply the seafloor every day causing seafloor damage and disrupting productive ecosystems.

The trajectory of global fish catch is well documented in government reports. UN Food and Agriculture Organisation (FAO) data indicate that in the mid-1970s 10 per cent of global fish catch was considered to be overfished, depleted or recovering. By 2006, that number was close to 30 per cent. To provide the full picture, it is also important to note that many global fisheries are considered data-deficient, meaning that we do not have adequate scientific information about catch levels, or in many cases, the life histories, migrations or spawning grounds of the species being harvested.

Perhaps the most telling indicator that we have hit the limit of continued growth of the global fishing enterprise is that the global catch of wild fish actually stopped growing in the mid-1980s and has remained level ever since. At the same time, the global seafood supply continues to ramp up, due the exponential growth of farmed seafood. Aquaculture has tremendous promise for global food security and as a source of economic growth for both developed and developing nations; however, it brings with it serious negative environmental consequences that must be addressed. A huge amount of wild fish is harvested for aquaculture feeds, with conversion ratios that don't make sense. Shrimp farms are being developed in fragile coastal areas like mangrove swamps that would be better left to provide coastal protection for local communities and a source of community-based fishing. Intensive aquaculture farms in enclosed coastal areas have caused nutrient pollution and local dead zones. Farmed fish pathogens have spread to native fish, and escaped fish are breeding with native strains, affecting their genetic make-up. It's clear that marine aquaculture is here to stay, but it must be done right. Fortunately, there is a growing movement to develop aquaculture standards and certification schemes to improve how seafood farming is done and assure consumers that its environmental impact is minimised.

The issues above are those that have been on the minds of scientists and environmental leaders for the past few decades. But today, we have a new and emerging issue to address that eclipses all others: global climate change. Climate change is clearly the biggest challenge humanity has faced in its history, and much progress has been made in identifying its causes and solutions. Unfortunately, to date, in nearly all of these conversations and actions, the oceans have been missing from the discussion. In truth, climate change is an ocean story. Our oceans absorb 22 million tons of CO_2 daily (over 21 million tonnes); this equates to them absorbing nearly half of the carbon emitted by humans over the last 200 years. They also absorb 80 per cent of the excess heat. In effect, we have the oceans to thank for buffering the effects of the vast amount of carbon we have put into the atmosphere in the last century. But the oceans have a limit to what they can absorb. Unfortunately we are now at a point where major changes are in store for our oceans due to carbon pollution. The most far-reaching is ocean acidification, caused by increased CO_2 levels changing ocean chemistry. This in turn will have huge impacts on the ocean food web and its myriad species that deposit calcium compounds to form their shells and body walls. Sea-level rise is of course a widely acknowledged problem, with major impacts on coastal human communities but also vast consequences for productive coastal wetlands. Sea warming has already been shown to have deleterious effects on coral reefs, and warming temperatures are already linked to species shifting to higher latitudes. And finally, changing ocean temperatures will change global current patterns, shifting weather and upwelling systems. To enable ocean ecosystems to endure these changes will require both mitigation – a commitment to reduce carbon pollution – and also healthy resilient ecosystems. If we can restore our oceans – end overfishing, wasted catch and unnecessary fishing subsidies, and create marine protected areas where marine life can thrive – we will have a chance of weathering the coming storm.

In reflecting on the state of our oceans and where to go next, it appears we are at a crossroads. The science is in: oceans need our help. We have the blueprint for restoring ocean health. What is standing in our way are human attitudes – complacency and lack of motivation to work towards a vision for a sustainable, healthy future that respects and protects human welfare *and* natural systems.

In running an aquarium, I have had a great deal of time to work with people and observe their attitudes. When I began, I thought the most challenging part of running an aquarium would be what happens on the wet side of the glass – the water systems, keeping the fish alive, working with new species. Over the years, I realised that the most challenging species in the aquarium was not the ocean animals, but the human animal. Understanding human motivation is the most important challenge before us. To get at this question, we have been engaged in a great deal of public opinion research, and it reflects some interesting results.

A recent opinion research study by The Ocean Project (www.theoceanproject.org) in 2009, examined public awareness and attitudes about climate change and the ocean. First, for members of the American public, not surprisingly, the environment is not a 'top-of-mind' concern and barely made it on to the list of top ten concerns in an open-ended question. The economy, health care, and other issues are far more important. Among environmental issues, the majority of respondents agree with the idea that climate change is the most important environmental issue confronting the world. When it comes to a link to oceans, however, the awareness is much lower. Most respondents can only name a few specifics about exactly how climate change will affect the ocean, with Americans only naming sea-level rise and creating more hurricanes. Despite the lack of awareness, though, there is a strong agreement with the statement 'When it comes to climate change, the actions of individual people can make a positive difference.' Americans agree there is an important role for the government in solving the climate change crisis, and even more so, a role for future technologies. A small sample of European respondents was included in this study but not published, and those results showed some interesting but not surprising differences between the US and European public. The European public has more knowledge about the issues, believes less in the power of personal action, more in the responsibility of government to solve the crisis and less in technology as an answer.

What do these results tell us? I believe they reflect the true crisis, which is a crisis of awareness and action. Our mission must be to redefine our relationship with the sea.

In my work leading a major public aquarium, I have seen many reasons to be optimistic. Our model, which I believe has merit for working with the public anywhere, is to inspire, engage and empower. I believe we must start by inspiring a connection with nature and ocean wildlife through our live animal exhibits or nature experiences. Then, we must engage people in learning more, through our interpretive exhibits at the aquarium or other learning activities. And finally, we must empower people to take action on the oceans' behalf. This means lifestyle choices that make a difference for ocean wildlife; taking personal responsibility to care for one's local environment; and engaging in the public process to shape government decisions about the oceans' future.

The most promising example of public action to improve ocean health is the growing seafood choices movement. Through consumer awareness programmes such as Monterey Bay Aquarium's Seafood Watch programme (www.seafoodwatch. org) consumers can access current information about sustainable seafood choices and vote with their wallets every time they dine or shop. This growing awareness has already led to results in the water. As an example, consumer action and media pressure to end overfishing of the Atlantic swordfish has led to reduced catch limits, and this fishery is now recovering. Major seafood buyers such as Walmart are working with NGOs to commit to sustainability standards for their seafood purchases, in turn affecting millions of pounds of wild and farmed seafood each year. The Marine Stewardship Council has established sustainability standards and a certification programme that has now certified dozens of fisheries with eco-labels so that consumers can buy seafood with confidence. A similar programme is underway for farmed seafood.

Along with consumer action, there are promising policy reforms underway. The US administration is developing a new national ocean policy to coordinate government oversight and ensure ecosystem protection is the central objective. New approaches to allocating fishing quotas are underway across the globe, and the idea of ocean zoning to better coordinate the growing number of ocean-users is gaining ground. The WTO is considering proposals to reduce fishing subsidies, which are contributing to overfishing in many parts of the world.

Finally, the growing designation of marine protected areas bodes well for the future. In coastal regions across the world, governments are designating special areas to protect from human impact so that ocean ecosystems can recover. In many regions, these marine reserves have been shown to be a benefit to nearby fishing communities, protecting healthy breeding populations of commercially valuable species and improving fish catch in adjacent waters. Scientists also point out that these protected areas provide resilience to help ocean ecosystems respond to the impacts of climate change and other perturbations. The International Union for the Conservation of Nature (IUCN) has set a goal to provide some sort of protected status for 20 to 30 per cent of our oceans; we are currently at less than 1 per cent.

So, what does the future hold for our oceans? The oceans of today face an escalating pace of competing uses by the 7 billion of us who take them for granted, as our species has for centuries. We look to them for food, energy resources, recreation, transportation, aquaculture and a host of new and growing enterprises. We have the tools to create a resilient ocean, which is what we need to do. We will need to invest more in science to better understand how Earth's natural systems work; we will need to reform fisheries policies; we will need to create protected areas now to ensure resilience and restore ecosystems for the future; and we will need to mobilise those of us in the developed world to vote with our wallets and get involved in change, as it is we who are driving the global fishing market in a way that is unjust and unsustainable.

In the end, our decisions now will have a profound impact on those who will come after us. As we consider the steps we will take to ensure a healthy future for our children, let us not forget the simple act of educating our children about the importance of caring for Earth's natural systems, on which we all depend. The Earth they inherit from us will be far from perfect, and we'll be leaving them a huge challenge. I'm encouraged by the momentum already underway.

Governance for Sustainability

NITIN DESAI

The Brundtland Commission's report *Our Common Future*, which inserted the notion of sustainable development into the global political discourse, states in the first sentence of the main text: 'The Earth is one but the world is not.'[1] The central task of governance for sustainability is to reconcile this contradiction and nowhere is this imperative more obvious than in the current struggle to cope with the challenge of climate change.

The concept of sustainable development seeks to connect different epistemic communities.[2] Its origins lie in the dialogue between ecologists and economists for formulating the World Conservation Strategy.[3] But in the Brundtland Commission it entered the policy discourse mainly as a way of providing a common framework for those sceptical about the merits of continued economic growth, and development advocates suspicious about the 'hidden agenda' of the, then, mainly western environmentalists.[4]

Over time other epistemic communities (lawyers, international relations theorists, natural scientists, urban planners and geographers) joined. Each of these communities finds deficiencies in the way sustainable development is typically defined. Each emphasises a different dimension of the concept as most relevant. Yet the concept provides a framework for a dialogue between disciplines such as land use planning, fishery and forestry with development economics.

A further connection is between activists and advocacy groups. Prior to the acceptance of sustainable development as the overarching goal, there was little by way of a dialogue between environmental activists, such as Greenpeace or Friends of the Earth, and developmental activists such as Oxfam. Sustainable development provides a shared framework for a meeting of these two agendas. Here, too, other activist communities such as women's groups, activists for children's right, indigenous people's rights and so on, have joined the conversation.

One difficulty with bridge concepts is that they do not belong to anybody on either shore. Hence there is always a certain tendency to harp on the deficiencies of the concept within the preferred framework of each discipline. There is also the usual charge that it is too vague. These criticisms will continue as long as sustainable development remains a foster-child in academia, governments and social activism. No university faculty or government department or NGO movement 'owns' this concept. For all of them it is simply a useful tool to increase their leverage with other disciplines in their sphere of action.

The situation can change if the concept is given greater precision in justifying actions proposed in its name. Now that the concept has acquired the status of a holy writ in policy dialogues the place to begin is to spell out the implications for governance of the three key operational dimensions of sustainable development: the ecological, the economic and the ethical.

First, the ecological dimension. Humans live and work in ecosystems, where the different components are interlinked in a complex web of dependencies. The geographical scale can range from neighbouring ecosystems to the Earth as a whole, and the timescale between cause and effect can stretch into decades or centuries. The reason for concern now is because the scale and depth of the human impact on ecosystems has increased enormously and we are closer to the thresholds and discontinuities that might lead to a sudden change.

The challenge for governance comes from the mismatch between sectoral and geographical jurisdictions and the trans-sectoral and trans-boundary character of ecosystem linkages. Climate change processes, for instance, are global and stretch well beyond the jurisdiction of the nation-states that exercise the sovereign power to make laws and policies. Action to manage and contain climate change risks requires the injection of climate concerns into the programmatic and policy agendas in a very wide range of economic sectors. That is the first challenge for governance – how inter-sectoral linkages and the fragmentation of jurisdictions can be taken into account in the fragmented structures of governance at the national and international level.

The second challenge is the economic dimension. Natural resources, along with produced capital, labour, knowledge and skills, are the basis for all economic activity. The way in which natural resources are used or abused is determined by the operation of profit maximising and utility maximising calculations of producers and consumers in a market economy. These seldom take into account the ecological interdependencies referred to above.

From an economic point of view, we can see these interdependencies as externalities, where one person's welfare depends on consumption decisions made by another and one entity's production possibilities are affected by the decisions made by another. From the perspective of sustainability, an externality of particular significance is the way in which one generation's choices constrain or enhance the options available to future generations.

The market-price mechanism does not provide the opportunity for all those who are affected, particularly those not yet born, to signal their preferences to others. The challenge for sustainability is that of designing economic instruments that correct these market failures.

The third is the ethical dimension. An environmental problem almost always involves an injustice between groups, regions and generations taking the form of an unrequited passing on of environmental costs to others. Redressing this requires a political process that is capable of enforcing the rights of those who lack market or political power and the obligations of those who have such power. The challenge is to express this ethical dimension in norms or legal principles that sufficiently constrain the exercise of power to protect the requirements of justice.

All three elements have to come together at the level of policies and programmes. Governance for sustainability will require that the border controls between disciplines are removed. Public policies and programmes will have to be designed and managed by a different type of person – one who is an ecologist who recognises that all interventions in natural systems need to be evaluated with a full understanding of the complex pathways through which local, national and global ecosystems are affected, enough of an economist to respect the need to compare costs and benefits and to recognise the potential of a properly managed market system to save us from the excesses and perversions of public control and also enough of an engineer or technologist to recognise that the right sort of development requires not just tweaking of the market, but a systematic effort to promote alternative technologies that are less aggressive in their use of natural systems. In all these, this person must be guided by the principle that the real test of development is what it does to the self-respect, dignity and well-being of the poorest person in society or, in the context of international relations, the least powerful state.

The response to global warming has to take account of all of these dimensions. Climate change involves ecological processes that link atmosphere, oceans and land resources in complex inter-actions. It is the mother of all externalities: global, long-term, highly variable in its impact in different geographies and involves risks of major irreversible changes in the ecosystems. It involves uncertainty because it is about realised externalities only to a limited extent and more about potential risks. It involves intra-generational equity because of large differences in impact in high latitudes/low latitudes, uplands/lowlands, coastal zones/inland areas, and more generally between rich and poor areas. Most importantly the causes and consequences stretch over decades and centuries and involve issues about intergenerational equity.

The basic facts are now more widely known[5] and can be summarised in two prognostications:

- A moderate increase of average global temperature by 2°C is already underway and probably unavoidable. It will affect hydrology, coastal zones, mountain ecosystems and biodiversity, with significant impacts on agriculture, health, settlements.

- A much larger potentially catastrophic increase of 5°C is possible if we continue with business as usual. Such a temperature increase will amplify impacts and create risks of activating tipping points, such as a large-scale Arctic ice melt, Greenland ice sheet melt, West Antarctic ice sheet melt, the release of methane from permafrost melt, and ocean temperature changes with effects on the Indian monsoon, El Niño and the Gulf Stream. Such a catastrophic increase can be prevented if action to mitigate greenhouse gas emissions is undertaken soon enough on a sufficient scale.

These prognoses involve three factors that our political processes are not well designed to handle. First, the time frame is long: most major impacts are projected to happen 50, even 100, years from now and the more catastrophic impacts even later than that. But action is required now if catastrophic impacts are to be avoided. Second, there is significant, but a gradually narrowing, scientific uncertainty about the projections. One thing worth noting is that each report prepared by the Intergovernmental Panel on Climate Change (IPCC)[6] has been more categorical in attributing the observed changes to human impact and more dire in its forecasts of impact. Third, those with the highest culpability as measured by cumulative contribution to greenhouse gas accumulations are least affected and some may even benefit from moderate increase. Those who are most affected are least culpable. They are also less developed and poorer and therefore less able to cope with the consequences.

Can democracies, as they function at present, cope with this challenge of taking decisions now to avert consequences in the distant future about which there is much uncertainty and which may affect people who are not voters at the time and in the jurisdictions where these decisions need to be taken?

In the liberal democracies of the West the reconciliation of democracy and a market economy has involved the acceptance of a role for public policy in free or subsidised provision of merit wants such as education and health care and underwriting a basic minimum of needs for all with a system of social welfare. It was this emergence of what was called the Welfare State in the United Kingdom, the New Deal in the USA, social democracy or the social market economy in Europe that made capitalism acceptable in the West. Environmental protection at home has been added to this agenda for some decades now.

Globalised capitalism lacks this underlying welfare consensus and the sense of solidarity and responsibility for the welfare of others is not extended to other nations. At the global level allocative outcomes are determined by market forces and distributive outcomes shaped by the interplay of political and economic power. This will not provide an adequate basis for effective, efficient and equitable action on climate change. We need a framework of principles similar to the one that led to capitalism with a human face in the West.

The frameworks and mindsets that shape policy need to be reconsidered and modified in four areas of concern:

- how we take account of the interests of future generations in today's decisions;

- the way we handle risk and uncertainty in our decisions;

- fairness in burden sharing between those who are most culpable and those who are worst affected; and

- ensuring concerted action by the 200 or so sovereign states that constitute the global economy.

A sense of responsibility to future generations is a part of most traditional value systems and is asserted in Principle 3 of the Rio Declaration on Environment and Development[7] *which states:* 'The right to development must be fulfilled so as to equitably meet developmental and environmental needs of present and future generations.' However, democratic societies work to a short-term calculus of costs and benefits because voters are myopic. The falling rate of savings in the West testifies to the growing preference for current consumption relative to future prosperity, possibly because of a rising proportion of older persons in the population. Greater awareness about potential impacts of climate change may help in restoring a respect for intergenerational equity. In the final analysis it will depend on how people value the welfare of those not yet born and the capacity of the political process to reflect this in day-to-day decisions.

Public policy decisions that are based on cost–benefit calculations do involve some valuation of the future relative to the present. The economic parameter that reflects this relative preference in cost–benefit analysis is the rate of time preference, or the rate at which income that will arise in the future is discounted relative to the same amount accruing today. One reason for such discounting is the expectation that income will be higher in the future and therefore any given amount is more valuable now when we are poorer than in the future when we will be richer. Another reason, referred to by economists as the pure rate of time preference, discounts future utility simply because it arises in the future. It is as if we were to say that a given amount of income accruing to our children is less valuable than the same amount accruing to us even if they are not any wealthier than we are. This may be understandable in an individual with a finite life, but not to a society that expects to survive forever. Hence public policy decisions must be based on a zero rate of pure time preference so that there is no discrimination between current and future generations when decisions have to be taken on resource conservation.

The uncertainty about the extent and timing of change is partly a function of the long time frame used for the projections and estimation of impacts. But the dynamics of climate change are such that the potential adverse impacts cannot be avoided unless we take action now. Whether this will happen will depend on how risk-averse we are. How will we balance out relatively low and uncertain probabilities of potential catastrophes far into the future with the near certainty of current costs?

In our present state of knowledge the downside risk of things turning out to be worse than expected seem to be greater than the chances of a pleasant surprise. The IPCC's current projections do not allow for the tipping points, like ice sheets melting or permafrost thaw or lower carbon absorption by oceans.[8] If things do not turn out to be quite as bad as expected, we can, to put it colloquially, start smoking again. But the reverse option of undoing past negligence is not available if things out to be worse than expected. In this situation even a risk-neutral society confronted by potential irreversible catastrophes should be prepared to bear some cost to keep options open for the future.

Precaution means caution in advance of full knowledge of the likelihood of damage. The celebrated precautionary principle, which is Principle 15 of the Rio Declaration, states: 'Where there are threats of serious or irreversible damage, lack of full scientific certainty shall not be used as a reason for postponing cost-effective measures to prevent environmental degradation.' This is the weak form of the principle, in that it seeks to balance the potential for damage against the costs of risk mitigation. The Stern Review of *The Economics of Climate Change*[9] estimates that the damage caused by inaction could amount to the equivalent of a 5 per cent consumption reduction now and forever, while the costs of mitigation to contain the risk of temperature increase to a 50:50 chance of staying below 2°C would cost an amount equivalent to a 1 per cent consumption reduction now and forever. This does not allow for catastrophic tipping points kicking in and, if this is taken into account, the damage from inaction could amount to a 20 per cent consumption reduction now and forever. On the basis of these numbers the case for taking out insurance and going beyond zero and low-cost measures seems justifiable.

This will not happen in the normal course. It will require policy interventions by way of public spending, incentives and regulatory changes by governments. But in democratic societies the immediate and measurable costs and benefits to voters and pressure groups trump any proposal to deploy public resources and policies to protect future options. This has to change and the implicit and explicit cost–benefit calculations that decision makers use must be modified to allow full play to the precautionary principle.

Who should bear the cost of this insurance? The damage from inaction and the cost of action are unevenly distributed between countries and generations. The technical and financial capacity to undertake mitigation actions is also unevenly distributed. There are two principles that UN member states have agreed in the Rio Declaration that are relevant. The first is 'the polluter should, in principle, bear the cost of pollution' (from Principle 16, Rio Declaration on Environment and Development) and the second (Principle 17), which is more explicit about global burden sharing:

> States shall cooperate in a spirit of global partnership to conserve, protect and restore the health and integrity of the Earth's ecosystem. In view of the different contributions to global environmental degradation, States have common but differentiated responsibilities. The developed countries acknowledge the responsibility that they bear in the international pursuit of sustainable development in view of the pressures their societies place on the global environment and of the technologies and financial resources they command.

The polluter pays and the common but differentiated responsibility principles clearly require that the costs of action should be distributed in proportion to culpability. The bulk of the accumulation of greenhouse gases since the industrial revolution is attributable to the industrial countries. Hence the Kyoto Protocol, where mitigation obligations are restricted to the industrial countries, is an application of the two principles. The Bali decisions go further and call for mitigation actions by developing countries but tie this to the provision of finance and technology by the industrial countries and, in that way, they remain within the bounds of the Rio Principles.

There is another aspect of burden sharing that needs cooperative action and that is adaptation to the changes that are unavoidable given any realistic goal for mitigation activity. If one looks at a world map, then the countries that have been most culpable in causing the problem, and hence the need for adaptation, are largely the industrial countries in the higher latitudes of the North. On the other hand, the countries that are most severely affected are developing countries in the lower latitudes. This is a case where the polluter pays principle can and should apply and the cost burden of adaptation should be borne by the industrial countries. The only issue is how much adaptation will be required – the less ambitious is the mitigation target, the greater is the burden of adaptation. In fact, one could argue that, if the Stern Review estimates of the costs of inaction are at all correct, the costs of adaptation will be far more substantial than the cost of vigorous and immediate action.

Now comes the difficult issue of the fragmented geography of sovereignty. The concern for future generations, the precautionary principle and fairness in burden sharing have to be given practical expression in the obligations to other jurisdictions that states recognise.

Governance must respond to the scale at which interdependence operates. Today we speak about global governance because economic, political and cultural linkages between communities cut across national boundaries. An individual's life chances depend not just on what is done in her community or country but also on the policies of other countries. Within the country an individual who lives in a democracy has the opportunity to influence the direction of policy. But there is no such direct influence that she has on the policies of the governments of other countries. There her influence has to operate through her government as it asserts and protects its national interest in global diplomacy.

Domestically, governance arrangements have evolved as the sovereignty of princes has given way to the sovereignty of people. Political power has been given a constitutional basis, rather than being simply seen as an absolute monarch's divine right to rule. The principle of people's sovereignty and people's representation has been accepted and reflected in political arrangements, very imperfectly of course in many cases. Domestic politics has evolved.

The politics of every country in the world looks different now from what it was just a couple of hundred years ago, and in many cases even from what it was 50 years ago.

But the way in which international relations are conducted does not look as different. There are some new institutions, many changes in the actual practice of diplomacy, greater knowledge and greater interaction. But the type of revolutionary transitions that have taken place in domestic governance, from absolutism to people's sovereignty, or in more recent times, from colonial subjugation to independence, have not taken place in the framework of international relations. The key changes at the domestic level – the development of constitutional rule, sovereignty rooted in law and the principle of citizen representation– do not have any counterpart at the global level.

The institutional and legal arrangements that have been made at the international level are better conceptualised as the analogue of a voluntary association. The principal institution of global governance, the United Nations, is founded on a paradox. Its charter begins with the words, 'We the people...'. But structurally it is not an association of people but a voluntary association of states represented by their executive branch. It is an organisation of nation-states that is meant to set standards and constrain the behaviour of these very states towards each other and towards their citizens. And even in this it has a limited impact as is seen in the impunity with which member states violate the principles and rules of behaviour incorporated in the Charter – non-aggression, avoiding the use of force except in self-defence, respect for human rights, and so on. Could it be that the world today is a confused mix of empire and a concert of nations, with both lacking any agreed constitutional basis, except for an inadequate UN Charter for the latter? Hegemony at the global level encourages regional hegemonies to appear, so that a type of global political feudalism is what we are moving to, but a feudalism with very poorly specified rights and obligations, a feudalism that is capricious and unpredictable.

This is clearly not the evolution that we are seeking. What we need to do is to recover the spirit of multilateralism and global cooperation that guided the establishment of the UN system. The fundamental goal of reform in the UN and other multilateral bodies must be to institute the changes that strengthen the role of basic constitutional principles and lessen the role of power.

But there are also issues of process. Global governance today faces a democracy deficit, a compliance deficit and a coherence deficit. The first is reflected in the sense of disempowerment felt by many developing-country governments, the second in the impunity with which states renege on their treaty obligations, and the third in the sectoral compartmentalisation of relations between states, both in the multilateral system and in the way in which external relations are organised within countries.

All three need to be addressed if we are to tackle the challenge of climate change and other global interdependencies. The UN Framework Convention on Climate Change provides a space for securing agreement. But the negotiating culture that drives this process is one founded on the classical model of reciprocal quid pro quo concessions. The nature of the climate challenge is such that it requires more than that, as participants have to agree on facts and projections, on the economics of the options available and a fair way of sharing the burden of concerted action.

Do we have a global political process that is capable of doing this? We do have an effective and democratic process in the IPCC and other networks of scientific cooperation for participants to agree on the data and the dynamics underlying projections and assessments of impact. The economics of climate change is now receiving much more systematic attention. The Stern Review has played a major role in raising the level of analysis and debate to a new level. But we do not as yet have a more structured process of consensus building in this area. The biggest gap, however, is in the third area of principles of fairness and burden sharing. What is missing is a perception by each participant that the others care for his interest, will reciprocate concessions and can be trusted to observe their commitments.

The climate process could be the beginning of a more effective mode of global environmental governance. Its impact could extend to other areas of interdependence because of its wide

sectoral ramifications. In the long run it could even be the start of
a new multilateralism. But that will require more than the perception of interdependence and mutual interest. The example of the
European Coal and Steel Community, which developed into the
European Union of today, points to the importance of persons in
positions of authority who have a long-term vision, of powerful
states recognising the concerns of smaller states, of credibility in
the eyes of people, as distinct from governments.

Governance for sustainability will require an epistemic change
in the way we view ourselves and our place in the world, so that
we look:

- *beyond nationalism* and recognise the realities of interdependence and the need to reflect this in partnerships within and
  between nations;
- *beyond interdependence* and accept that our obligations to each
  other cannot be defined solely by mutual interests but require
  mutual responsibility or solidarity;
- *beyond individualism* and look at progress not just as individual
  advancement but as the advancement of the common good
  of the community.

Notes

1 World Commission on Environment and Development, *Our Common
   Future* (Oxford: Oxford University Press, 1987).
2 An epistemic community is one that seeks to understand and explain
   a specified set of phenomena, for instance the behaviour of elementary particles or of prices in a market, with a generally shared
   methodology of observation, experiment, explanation and proof.
3 International Union for the Conservation of Nature (IUCN), *World
   Conservation Strategy* (Gland: IUCN, 1980), accessible at http://
   data.iucn.org/dbtw-wpd/edocs/WCS-004.pdf.
4 This is based on the author's direct involvement in the drafting of the
   report of the Brundtland Commission, particularly the first two chap-
   ters of the main report.
5 A very useful one-stop article on global warming is at http://en.
   wikipedia.org/wiki/Global_warming.
6 The IPCC was established in 1988 by the World Meteorological

Organisation and the United Nations Environment Programme and is open to all their member countries. The IPCC provides at regular intervals comprehensive, rigorously documented Assessment Reports that summarise the current knowledge and future projections of climate change (CC). 'Climate Change 2007' is the fourth IPCC Assessment Report (AR4). The previous ones were published in 1990, 1995 and 2001. AR4 involved 800 contributing authors, 450 lead authors and 2,500 scientific expert reviewers. Its authoritative reports are available at http://www.ipcc.ch.

7 United Nations, *Rio Declaration on Environment and Development* (Geneva: United Nations, 1992), accessible at http://www.un.org/documents/ga/conf151/aconf15126-1annex1.htm.

8 IPCC, 'Summary for Policymakers', in S. Solomon et al. (eds), *Climate Change 2007: The Physical Science Basis. Contribution of Working Group I to the Fourth Assessment Report of the Intergovernmental Panel on Climate Change* (Cambridge: Cambridge University Press, 2007).

9 N.S. Stern et al., *Stern Review: The Economics of Climate Change* (London: HM Treasury, 2006).

Climate Change:
The Perspective from Europe

ALEX ELLIS

You may well be wondering what on earth the British ambassador to Portugal is doing contributing to a conference on climate change. Well, I had a previous life and I worked for a few years with the President of the European Commission, trying to turn knowledge into reality and listening to the public policy reality. And I learnt a bit about how you get European leaders to agree to ideas to achieve this, to turn knowledge into public policy.

So, I've got a little knowledge, but I'm not a scientist – I have all the profound knowledge of climate change that a medieval history specialism allows you to have. The second thing to remember, if you forget everything else, is that if we consider what the world looks like with a temperature increase of 4°C up from pre-industrial levels, then it's not great news and it's really, really not great news for quite large chunks of Portugal. This is going to have a very significant effect on Portugal and I suspect on your lives and not just yours, on many others as well.

So, while I personally may not know much about climate change, my team in the Embassy does. Every year the British Foreign Office gives awards to the greenest embassies in the world, and we were nominated this year.

We're growing vegetables, among other things, and even offered a selection to the Secretary of State for the Environment, Humberto Rosa. As a result of our initiatives we have reduced our water consumption in the Embassy, in one year, by 30 per cent and reduced our electricity consumption by 8 per cent. I think that, in fact, British leadership and successive British prime ministers have taken this issue seriously and have been working with the rest of the world to take this issue seriously.

Can a Brit really talk about Europe? Well, I am European, and the fact is the European policy on climate change owes a great deal to Tony Blair and to Gordon Brown and I have no shame in saying that. I think it has been a great achievement by those two leaders.

I want to discuss Europe, how it got to where it got to on climate change, and the world in fact got less Westphalian; and I've got a nasty feeling it may start to become more Westphalian in the future rather than less. Put another way, I think we got less nationalistic and now we're about to get more nationalistic. This quote comes from the Messina Declaration, one of the very first things that Europe ever said about anything, when some of the leaders of Europe were getting together in 1955. In other words, at the heart of the idea of the European Union was the idea of sharing sovereignty on energy; it was one of the most basic things and it was driven very much at the time by nuclear energy. I believe it was one of the first ideas on which European leaders came together, regarding what we should cooperate on: to cooperate on nuclear energy. Putting more abundant nuclear energy at a cheaper price at the disposal of European economies is very much at the core of what Europe is, but there's one huge concept missing in all this: you don't see the word 'sustainability' anywhere, you don't see the word 'environment' in there, anywhere. In other words, when European leaders were thinking about the world in 1955, they were not thinking about the environment.

And for a long time, energy disappeared off the European map, so much so that I think that if you look at the Constitutional Treaty, the Lisbon Treaty, it's hardly referred to at all. So, energy kind of disappeared, but environment came in in a big way. First of all in the Single European Act (1986) and then in the Maastricht Treaty

(1992). In other words, you had a very rapid evolution of environmental policy.

What's been happening in the last few years is an attempt to join climate change and energy together and this has happened in a big way. Why is that? Basically, it's because of climate change, because of the reality of climate change, because of the science of climate change.

At the same time we also had the energy crisis, for the very reason that it was considered a good thing to be 'abundant at a cheaper price'. The fact is, energy in EU is getting less abundant and it's getting more expensive, and that is for a number of reasons. This has been brought to a head by the disputes between Russia and Ukraine over the supply of gas to roughly a third of the European countries, so what happened over the last few years is the creation of what people tend to refer to as the Lisbon–Kyoto–Moscow Triangle: Moscow for energy supply, Kyoto for climate change, Lisbon in the terms of the Lisbon Process about competitive economy. There's another reason why Europe wants to deal with climate change and that's because of the nature of the EU itself.

First of all, Europeans like action on climate change. Look at the eurobarometer, for example, the European public opinion surveys; climate change is back at the top of the list of things people think the EU should be dealing with.

The very nature of the problem of climate change is also attractive to Europeans because it crosses borders. Everyone is in the same boat, and so, in a way, it is part of the existential justification for the EU. Why do we get so interested in climate change, in energy and the Lisbon–Kyoto–Moscow Triangle? Well, short-term politics come into this a lot. During 2005, there were 'No' votes to the Constitutional Treaty from France and from the Netherlands, a big crisis, followed by a failure to agree about the future of the European Budget. Some blamed the United Kingdom. So Tony Blair tried to relaunch ideas around the development of the EU at a Summit in Hampton Court in late 2005, and one of the areas he picked up was energy, a European energy grid, a good idea. He provided political momentum to this. Roughly at the same time my former boss, the President of the European Commission, became very interested in these issues, partly, I have to say, as the result of conversations with people who are sitting here today, and so the Commission came up with some proposals, known as the 20/20/20 package, which European leaders agreed to: a reduction of greenhouse gases of 20 per cent by 2020 and an increase in energy efficiency of 20 per cent by 2020 and an increase in renewable energy to 20 per cent of the energy mix by 2020.

That experience taught me a couple of things that may or may not be relevant in the case of the Copenhagen process. The first was, you enlarge the problem in order to find a solution. If we had simply tried as the EU to reach an agreement on the Kyoto target at 20 per cent, we might have succeeded, but we might not – because to be absolutely honest, some countries in the EU do not care very much about climate change. Some do. But among those who don't, some really care about energy security and the possibility of increasing their own indigenous energy supply, so they were very attracted by some of the parts of the package which would decrease Europe's growing import dependency. And virtually all the countries are worried about spikes in energy prices and looking for ways in which you can try to have a more effective energy market within the EU. So the problem gets enlarged and you find a solution, and this is, I think, what happened.

It also required a great deal of political negotiation at the very last moment. I remember President Barroso standing and talking to the then Czech prime minister, the Slovak prime minister, then the Hungarian. And we were having a very, very fast negotiation – about two years of work went into about three minutes of negotiation!

So, what we are going to do now? Europe is absolutely leading in wanting to have an ambitious deal for Copenhagen and has got the most ambitious targets there are for Copenhagen. Why? Because of the science; because, I think, the consequences of climate change for the environment, for security, are becoming very evident.

So far so good. So far, a European world, where Europe decides. But the truth of the matter is, there's a huge elephant in the room, it's what we all know: Europe produces, I think, around 15 per cent of the world's greenhouse gas emissions. In other words, what European leaders think is nowhere near enough to deal with the issue of climate change.

I heard the other day that 97 per cent of the emissions growth by 2020 will come from the developing world, and this is a real problem for Europe, not just in climate change but more generally. How on earth do you convince the rest of the world to do what you want it to do? And that's the big challenge for Europeans in many areas of public policy.

There are some answers to that. First of all you must show that your policies work and European policies on greenhouse gas emissions have worked! We have grown, our economies have grown and our greenhouse gas emissions have fallen; European GDP has grown by roughly 45 per cent since 1990, and the emissions were down, I think, about 16 per cent in 2007. In the UK they went down by 18 per cent.

Now, it could be better, it should be better, but we are respecting the Kyoto commitments. So, the policy works, and policies and the models which they create have a significant influence, more than we think sometimes. We heard that from David King, yesterday morning: he gave an example of how European GMO policy is, in his view, causing people to die in India and the Philippines; so Europe shouldn't underestimate the power of European policies.

I think it's really important for Europeans to actually reach agreements and to stick to them, for example on climate change financing. Because when Europe acts, others tend to define their position against and around Europe's.

And I think in our negotiating approach we have to be positive; we have to say we will go further. I think we have to be more absolutist, rather than say, 'Well, I would do this, but if you won't, I can't.' I think Europe has to work with other countries outside the EU, on technology, for example, and to use our policy instruments not as sticks but as carrots.

In other words, we should be giving more tariffs incentives, in my view, to countries that are going in the direction we would like them to go on greenhouse gases, just as we do for countries that sign and respect International Labour Organisation conventions. Why don't we do the same in the environment? We should try to incentivise good environmental behaviour through our market, because the European market is huge, and we should be using the power of our standards to try to raise standards around the world. I think of the Energy Star programme, the American programme that has led to computers consuming less energy. And I think we can now emphasise our greenhouse gas emissions reduction offer by saying we will cut them by 20 per cent and we will go to 30 per cent if others do as well.

Finally, two more things: Europeans can contribute to science; and Europe shouldn't preach to the rest of the world. Climate change is an issue on which I've heard more preaching than any other policy issue. Preaching doesn't work. Countries like the USA, or India or China, will do what we the Europeans would like them to do, not because we would like them to do it, but because they want to do it, because they are perceiving it to be in their own interest, that this is what is good for them and what is good for the world. Now, how do you marry those different visions together? It's a huge challenge, but really there's nothing like the science to help you along the way, to show you why it is worth doing this.

So far, so good. We can imagine a scenario at Copenhagen where people have their own interests, but there's a kind of collective will, a sense that we need to do something, we need to reduce greenhouse gas emissions, we need to get commitments from China, from the USA, maybe, who knows, from India, saying we will do our bit, too, we need to do more and so forth.

But I think there's a big, big but in all of this, and this is the thought I would like to leave with you. Europeans like the European kind of world; they like the world in which everyone behaves a bit like Europe, where you pool sovereignty, where you have a supranational body which is the only one that can propose laws and can hold you to account, where you have a court which can fine you if you don't respect those laws. But is the rest of the world ever going to follow that model, I wonder?

There are two gorillas, I think I can call them gorillas, each emitting over 20 per cent of global greenhouse gases emissions, the USA and China, and they might both be prepared through very, very different governance mechanisms to say, we will reduce greenhouse gas emissions substantially and here are some targets; but now, are these really two countries which are prepared to have any kind of multilateral supervision to call them to account for that?

Europe cannot do it alone; there's no way it can do it alone, so climate change goes to a bigger organisation, in this case the United Nations. Europe may say, we have done it. The others may say yes, I will do it … but in the end we will decide whether we've done it or not, and no one else will have any control over that.

We could get that outcome, maybe we'll get it at Copenhagen. Maybe it's OK to get that outcome, to say it's the end that matters and the end is controlling the increase of greenhouse gas emissions into the atmosphere. But if we do that without supranational control, in a way we make the world more nationalistic instead of less nationalistic and I think there are some risks and a price to be paid for that in the longer run.

Climate Change Politics
under Barack Obama

MIRANDA SCHREURS

With the election of Barack Obama, climate change is back on the agenda in the USA. After a long period of anti-Kyoto politics during the George W. Bush administration, the USA is showing numerous signs of a willingness to re-engage with international climate negotiations. Since taking office in January 2009, Barack Obama has been working to re-engage the USA in the international environmental debate.

Climate Initiatives during the Bush White House

George W. Bush's first major international policy act as President of the United States was to withdraw from the Kyoto Protocol. Responding to his conservative base, he villainised the Kyoto Protocol, calling it a potential job-killer and bad for economic growth. Bush questioned the accuracy and scientific consensus behind climate change, regularly calling for more research into the matter.

Less well-known are the policy measures he introduced to try to quell the international and domestic uproar his anti-Kyoto politics instigated. The main policy change was his introduction of a voluntary greenhouse gas intensity target, that is, a reduction in the amount of energy required to produce a unit of gross domestic product (GDP) to 18 per cent of 2002 levels by 2012. This target basically equates to an energy efficiency improvement target. It is the kind of target now being embraced by China and India.

The greenhouse gas intensity target was set relatively low and as a result did not to lead to any reduction in aggregate greenhouse gas emissions. Although between 2002 and 2007, greenhouse gas intensity dropped by an average of 2.1 per cent per year and there was a total emissions intensity reduction of 9.8 per cent and a general stabilisation in emissions levels, emissions were 14.5 per cent higher in 2007 than 1990 (see Table below).[1]

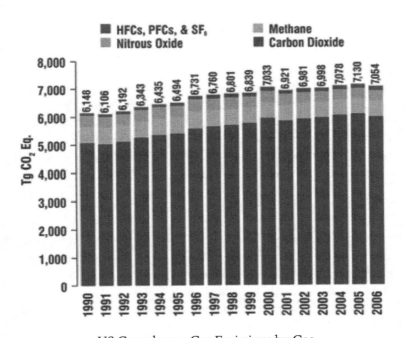

US Greenhouse Gas Emissions by Gas

(Source: http://www.epa.gov/climatechange/emissions/usgginventory.html)

Beyond this, the Bush administration focused some attention on research and development of new technologies. They introduced a climate change technology programme, a climate change science programme and a hydrogen fuel initiative.

The Bush White House also focused attention on the big emitting states of the developing world, pointing out that in the future China would be the world's largest greenhouse gas emitter (a status it won in 2007). In an effort to forge a path distinct from that being pursued through the United Nations based Kyoto Protocol, the Bush White House began to pursue bilateral and smaller regional climate dialogues. An important initiative in this area was the Asia Pacific Partnership on Clean Development and Climate Change. This linked the USA with Australia, Canada, China, Japan, India and South Korea in a cooperative partnership focused on technological solutions to climate change.

Barack Obama: Forging a New Path

Barack Obama clearly distanced himself from the Bush White House on environmental matters during his election campaign. Obama accused the Bush administration of a 'stubborn refusal' to tackle climate change and argued that 'unless we free ourselves from a dependence on these fossil fuels and chart a new course on energy in this country, we are condemning future generations to global catastrophe'.[2] At various points during his campaign, Obama spelled out his plans for a different energy path and a different set of climate change policies.

Obama and the Green New Deal: Linking the Financial Crisis, Energy Security and Climate Protection

Soon after being elected into office, Obama linked his interest in a new development path to the nation's economic and financial problems. In a 21 November 2008 speech Obama spelled out his vision for a Green New Deal.

[I]t will be a two-year, nationwide effort to jumpstart job creation in America and lay the foundation for a strong and growing economy. We'll put people back to work rebuilding our crumbling roads and bridges, modernising schools that are failing our children, and building wind farms and solar panels, fuel-efficient cars and the alternative energy technologies that can free us from our dependence on foreign oil and keep our economy competitive in the years ahead.

It is time for America to lead again. Thanks to our recovery plan, we will double this nation's supply of renewable energy in the next three years... We will soon lay down thousands of miles of power lines that can carry new energy to cities and towns across this country. And we will put Americans to work making our homes and buildings more efficient so that we can save billions of dollars on our energy bills. But to truly transform our economy, to protect our security and save our planet from the ravages of climate change, we need to ultimately make clean, renewable energy the profitable kind of energy.

So I ask this Congress to send me legislation that places a market-based cap on carbon pollution and drives the production of more renewable energy in America.... And to support – to support that innovation, we will invest $15 billion a year to develop technologies like wind power and solar power, advanced biofuels, clean coal, and more efficient cars and trucks built right here in America.[3]

In his speech, Obama was working to alter the image of climate change protection from the perspective pushed by the Bush administration, which was that climate change would be costly in terms of jobs and harmful for economic growth, to an image of climate change action as an opportunity for change, new jobs and a brighter, cleaner, more modern and independent energy future.

Responding to Pressures from Cities, States and Regions

Barack Obama's embrace of climate change issues, renewable energy and energy efficiency certainly have been influenced by the strong demands for change that have been emanating from urban and rural communities, states and regions.

Early Signs of Change: The 2006 Congressional Elections and the 110th Congress

There is little doubt that the USA will become more proactively engaged in international environmental issues in the next years. Pressures are coming from multiple fronts. The 2006 mid-term Congressional elections swept a Democratic majority into both Houses of Congress. The 110th Congress began holding hearings on climate change and pushing for changes in US energy policy already in the run-up to the presidential election. One of the biggest environmental successes of 2007 was the passage of the Energy Independence and Security Act, which raises the overall fuel economy of cars and light trucks to 35 miles per gallon by 2020. The bill passed on a vote of 264 to 163 with 8 not voting in the House of Representatives, and in the Senate by a vote of 65 to 27 with 7 not voting.[4] Although comprehensive global warming legislation did not reach the floor of either the House or the Senate in the final years of the Bush presidency, there was a non-binding Sense of the Senate on Climate Change resolution that expresses the sense of the Senate that the country should take mandatory steps to slow, stop and reverse the growth of greenhouse gas emissions:

> It is the sense of the Senate that Congress should enact a comprehensive and effective national program of mandatory, market-based limits and incentives on emissions of greenhouse gases that slow, stop, and reverse the growth of such emissions at a rate and in a matter that—a.) will not significantly harm the United States economy; and b.) will encourage comparable action by other nations that are major trading partners and key contributors to global emissions.[5]

Pressures from Below: Cities and States Mobilise for Climate Action

There has been a surge of climate change activity at the local and state levels in the USA. In fact, the USA has become something of a hotbed of experimentation with climate change protection policies and programmes at the local, municipal, state and regional levels.

The municipal level The US Conference of Mayors adopted a Climate Protection Agreement that now has close to 1,000 signatures. Participating cities have agreed to adopt Kyoto-type targets to reduce their greenhouse gas emissions. These include policies to prevent sprawl, promote alternative transportation and purchase cleaner energy and more efficient appliances, among many others. In addition, they have agreed to urge the federal and state governments to adopt emissions trading systems.

The state level Numerous states have introduced climate change legislation. Oregon, for example, passed legislation that states it shall be a goal of the state to stabilise greenhouse gas levels at 1990 levels by 2010 and to reduce them by 10% of 1990 levels by 2020 and 75% of 1990 levels by 2050. Colorado has a target of 20% below 2005 levels by 2020 and 80% below 2005 levels by 2050.

California California has been particularly active. California's AB 32, the Global Warming Solutions Act of 2006, set a state-wide CO_2 emissions target: stabilisation of emissions at 1990 levels by 2020 (which is equivalent to a 30 per cent below business-as-usual projection, given California's rapidly expanding population). The California Pavley Bill (AB 1493) introduced requirements that new vehicles sold in the state achieve 'maximal feasible reduction' of CO_2 emissions, basically pressuring automobile manufacturers to reduce the carbon emissions of their entire fleet. Car makers were given until 2009 to meet the new standards. Although in December 2007 the Bush administration rejected the bill as going beyond California's competence, as one of his first acts as President, in January 2009 Obama ordered the Environmental Protection Agency to revisit the Bush-era ruling.

The regional level About half of the 50 states have entered into regional climate change and emission trading pacts. In April 2003, New York Governor George Pataki initiated the idea of a regional cap-and-trade programme for the region stretching from Maine to Maryland. In late 2005, an agreement to implement the Regional Greenhouse Gas Initiative was reached. Membership has expanded to include ten states: Connecticut, Delaware, Maine, Maryland, Massachusetts, New Hampshire, New Jersey, New York, Rhode Island and Vermont. In addition, the District of Columbia, Pennsylvania, Ontario, Quebec, the Eastern Canadian Provinces and New Brunswick are observers to the process. The idea of the regional cap-and-trade programme is to help states meet the individual greenhouse gas emissions reduction goals they have formulated. Other regional initiatives have taken root as well, including the Midwestern Regional Greenhouse Gas Reduction Accord, Energy Security and Climate Stewardship Platform for the Midwest, Western Climate Initiative, Western Governors' Association (WGA): Clean and Diversified Energy Initiative, and Powering the Plains.

These trends are certainly attributable at least in part to the failure of the federal government in Washington, DC under the Bush administration (2000–2008) to play a strong leadership role in climate change politics. Frustrated by national intransigence and the decision of the Bush administration to withdraw from the Kyoto Protocol, many local and state governments started to take action on their own.

New Policy Directions

In his New Energy for America Plan, Obama called for cutting carbon emissions by 80 per cent by 2050, putting 1 million plug-in hybrids that can get up to 150 miles per gallon on the road by 2015, and ensuring that 10 per cent of our electricity comes from renewable sources by 2012 and 25 per cent by 2025.[6] Obama has indicated his willingness to consider nuclear energy, but has also called for first addressing the public right-to-know, security of nuclear fuel and waste, waste storage, and proliferation. Obama has opposed offshore oil drilling.

In response to the demands for a stimulus package to deal with the ailing economy, Obama pushed for a green stimulus package, one that would inject public funds into the economy, but in large part to support green infrastructure development, investment and jobs. The American Investment and Recovery Act includes support for smart grid technology, which enables more efficient electricity transmission and better management of renewable energy. It provides a federal matching grant programme for smart technology projects and supports research and development in carbon capture and storage technology. It promotes energy efficiency improvement, alternative fuel trucks and buses, smart and energy efficient appliances, advanced vehicle battery research, renewable energy research and development, and environmental clean-up of cold war nuclear waste, among many other initiatives.

The House of Representatives: The American Clean Energy and Security Act of 2009 (the Waxman-Markey Bill)

The American Clean Energy and Security Act of 2009 (H.R. 2454), also known for its main authors, Henry Waxman and Edward Markey (the Waxman-Markey Bill) narrowly passed in the House of Representatives by a vote of 219 to 212 with 3 representatives present, but not voting.[7] It is the most important climate legislation being considered in the 111th Congress. It has four titles. Title I addresses a federal renewable electricity standard, carbon capture and storage technology, performance standards for new coal-fuelled power plants, a low carbon fuel standard and smart grid advancement. Title II deals with efficiency standards for mobile sources and other transportation programmes. Title III proposes a cap-and-trade programme with economy-wide coverage of emissions sources over 25,000 tons (22,750 tonnes) per year, and emissions caps that would reduce aggregate greenhouse gas emissions for all covered entities to 3% below their 2005 levels in 2012, 20% below 2005 levels in 2020, 42% below 2005 levels in 2030, and 83% below 2005 levels in 2050. Title IV deals with domestic competitiveness and support for workers, assistance to consumers and support for domestic and international adaptation initiatives while transitioning to a clean energy economy. For a climate bill of this kind to come into law, the Senate must first pass its own climate bill and then the two bills must be brought together in Committee.

The Senate: The Clean Energy Jobs and American Power Act (the Kerry-Boxer Bill)

In the Senate, the counterpart to the Waxman-Markey Bill is S. 1733, Clean Energy Jobs and American Power Act, introduced by Senators John Kerry and Barbara Boxer and commonly known as the Kerry-Boxer Bill. The bill speaks to the themes Obama has been pushing:

Congress finds that –
1) the United States can take control of the energy future of the United States, strengthen economic competitiveness, safeguard the health of families and the environment, and ensure the national security of the United States by increasing energy independence;
2) creating a clean energy future requires a comprehensive approach that includes support for the improvement of all energy sources, including coal, natural gas, nuclear power, and renewable generation;
3) efficiency in the energy sector also represents a critical avenue to reduce energy consumption and carbon pollution, and those benefits can be captured while generating additional savings for consumers;
4) substantially increasing the investment in the clean energy future of the United States will provide economic opportunities to millions of people in the United States and drive future economic growth in this country;
5) the United States is responsible for many of the initial scientific advances in clean energy technology, but, as of September 2009, the United States has only 5 of the top 30 leading compa-

nies in solar, wind, and advanced battery technology;
6) investment in the clean energy sector will allow companies
in the United States to retake a leadership position, and the jobs
created by those investments will significantly accelerate
growth in domestic manufacturing.

The bill goes on to note areas where job creation can be expected,
the positive health impacts that can be expected from reducing
pollution, and the potential to reduce energy price volatility that
impacts on the low-income families of the country most. It also
talks about the threats that climate change pose to the country.[8]

The main proposal of the bill is a cap-and-trade system that goes
beyond that set in the Waxman-Markey Bill: a 20 per cent reduction of greenhouse gas emissions by 2020 and an 80 per cent
reduction by 2050 relative to 2005 levels. The bill is meeting some
fierce opposition in the Senate, however, so its prospects remain
uncertain.

Voices of Opposition

Efforts to reframe the climate debate have had some success. The
Obama White House has succeeded to some extent in portraying
climate change as a serious problem, but one with solutions that
can result in new jobs, new industries and a cleaner future. The
Obama team has had some success in policy change, having
defined carbon dioxide as a pollutant, raised fuel efficiency standards for automobiles and targeted millions in spending for
renewable energies, energy efficiency and research related to
climate change. Opposition to the Obama climate programmes
and to the Copenhagen international climate negotiations,
however, is still strong. The National Association of Manufacturers and the National Federation of Independent Businesses
launched a broadcast, radio and Internet advertising campaign to
oppose the Waxman-Markey cap-and-trade bill. The conservative
media is supporting an anti-Al Gore documentary, *Not Evil Just
Wrong: The True Cost of Global Warming Hysteria*. The coal and oil

industries have launched large-scale efforts to block Obama's climate change policy strategy. An email from the American Petroleum Institute outlined its plans to organise citizen rallies in 20 states against Obama's climate programmes. This suggests that Obama's efforts to reframe the debate are meeting with substantial opposition from some powerful players. This, of course, also has an impact on Congressional debate where Congressmen, both Republican and Democrat, from coal- and oil-producing states are being pressured to oppose the climate change bills being debated in Congress.

Conclusion

With Obama in the White House, the USA is certain to be more engaged in international environmental negotiations and to have a more active environmental programme than it did during the past decade. Eventually, Congress is likely to present new energy legislation that further promotes energy efficiency improvements and renewable energy, the introduction of a cap-and-trade programme, stronger support for environmental and energy research and development, and stronger restrictions on chemicals. Of course, with Obama in office and a Democrat-controlled Congress, expectations will be high for an activist and 'green' politics. This may result in a certain level of disillusionment if the Obama team is unable to deliver satisfactory answers to international partners at the Copenhagen climate summit in December 2009. It is unlikely that the US Congress will be able to pass climate legislation prior to some time in 2010. Still, there is little doubt that the Obama team has been reframing the climate debate, and in the process opening new potentials for change.

Notes

1 From the *Inventory of US Greenhouse Gas Emissions and Sinks: 1990–2006, USEPA 430-R-08-005.*
2 Barack Obama, 'Energy Independence and the Safety of Our Planet', speech, 3 April 2006, http://obamaspeeches.com/060-Energy-

Independence-and-the-Safety-of-Our-Planet-Obama-Speech.htm.

3 Text of Obama's Radio Address, *New York Times*, 22 November 2008.

4 H.R. 6: Energy Independence and Security Act of 2007. See http://www.govtrack.us.

5 Senate Amendment 866 to the Energy Policy Act of 2005 (H.R. 6).

6 Speech text: 'Barack Obama and Joe Biden: New Energy for America'. See http://www.barackobama.com/pdf/factsheet_energy_speech_080308.pdf.

7 H.R. 2454: American Clean Energy and Security Act of 2009. See http://www.govtrack.us.

8 S. 1733, Clean Energy and American Power Act.

Prospects for a Sustainable Future

JONATHON PORRITT

This timely and significant Conference has reminded us, very powerfully, of the scale and urgency of the multiple environmental challenges we now face – on fresh water, oceans, agriculture, forestry, biodiversity and so on. While it may now be true that climate change dominates the policy agenda, the simple conclusion arising from all of these Conference contributions is that humankind would be heading towards a horrifically painful series of ecological disasters *even if climate change was not underway*. Even without accelerating climate change, humankind now stands on the brink of catastrophe.

That's a pretty startling conclusion. In effect, it means that 45 years on from the publication of Rachel Carson's *Silent Spring* (which is seen by many as marking the birth of modern environmentalism), we've actually made very little progress in addressing these challenges. Global treaties and national regulations have helped slow the pace of destruction, but the combined momentum of rapid population growth and even more rapid growth in the scale of the economy has ensured a continuing war of attrition against the natural world.

In the early days, any real understanding of the cumulative impact of that 'momentum for destruction' was limited. The research base was itself limited. Public awareness was patchy, and largely issue-specific. Political will was all but invisible. The Limits to Growth hypothesis in the early 1970s was seen off by a consortium of cornucopians in business, politics and academia. The 'truth' about the state of the world did not 'set us free' in terms of empowering politicians to change course.

By 1992, at the time of the Earth Summit in Rio de Janeiro, such excuses were no longer available to decision makers. The consequences of continuing on a 'business-as-usual' basis had been fully laid out in the 1987 Brundtland Report, *Our Common Future*, and these were captured even more eloquently in the raft of global statements and agreements that emerged from the Earth Summit itself. From that point on, what we have done (or what we have failed to do) has been done or not done with knowledge aforethought. And that changes the whole ethical basis by which we should hold our world leaders to account.

Meanwhile, the war of attrition goes on. The truth about the state of the world has still not set us free. Rich countries fare better because they have more money to spend on cleaning up the mess. Poor countries stick to that all too familiar FROG mantra (First Raise Our Growth). Pollution, resource depletion and the accelerating loss of biodiversity are all still seen as the regrettable but 'acceptable' price to be paid for economic progress.

This kind of systemic trade-off (trading off our 'natural capital' for rising material plenty) remains *the* dominant hallmark of what we mean by 'progress' today. And were it not for accelerating climate change, I am not at all sure what would have broken this cycle of mutually assured destruction. The Faustian rationale behind that model of progress, however perverse it may be, is still almost universally accepted as the best model available to us. That's just the way it's been, and the way it still is.

From that somewhat world-weary perspective, the galvanising effect of accelerating climate change on global politics could be interpreted as a just-in-time game-changer. The threat is so serious, the science so robust and the potential consequences so grim, that our politicians can no longer turn that same well-exercised blind eye as they have done to every other symptom of unsustainable economic growth. Accelerating climate change is unignorable. It demands their full and urgent attention – today, not tomorrow.

It may be unwise to push this too far, but I cannot help but believe that without climate change materialising so dramatically in our lives (in the lives of *all* people, wherever they live, whether they appreciate it or not) as an unignorable reality, we would still be trucking along trashing the planet in every other respect as if there were, quite literally, no tomorrow. That game-changing reality may therefore be represented as a rather weird silver lining to the very dark cloud of accelerating climate change – and I shall return to that later.

Climate change may be unignorable for the scientists and even for the vast majority of politicians, but it is still easily ignored by very large numbers of people today. Given what we now know about what is actually happening on the ground as a direct consequence of accelerating climate change, regardless of what today's computer models do or do not tell us, this refusal to engage on the part of so many people in so many countries seems at first sight to be incomprehensible.

What do I mean by that? Opinion polls in many different countries demonstrate that significant percentages of people remain sceptical about the science of climate change, unimpressed by the response of their politicians, and still uncertain about whether or not they themselves, as individual citizens, can do anything to make any kind of difference. In the UK and USA in particular, polls in the last quarter of 2009 revealed fewer people were persuaded by the science of climate change than was the case at the end of 2008.

Looking at that kind of data, even those who are still optimistic about humankind rising to the challenge of accelerating climate change have to acknowledge that there are going to have to be some traumatic shocks to the system, induced by climate change, to jolt politicians and their electorates the world over to move up a gear. These shocks will come, inevitably, and from the perspective of our long-term prospect as a species, they need to come as rapidly as possible. And they need to be as traumatic as possible – otherwise politicians and their electorates will rapidly revert to the current mix of doubt, non-specific anxiety and inertia.

Public opinion in the USA after Hurricane Katrina provides perhaps the best example of this phenomenon. Initially, there was a substantial surge in levels of public interest and concern. However, it took just two years for Fox News and other right-wing shock-jocks to straighten out deviant US citizens who had started to think it really might be time for their nation to get stuck in on climate change.

Australia provides an even more compelling example of just how difficult the politics of climate change really are. Over the last few years, Australia has had more than its fair share of traumatic shocks, in terms of devastating droughts, the near-collapse of agriculture in the Murray-Darling Basin (where river flows in some places are down to 5 per cent of their long-term average), increasingly severe bush fires and heatwaves, and worsening damage to the Great Barrier Reef – the symbolic heartland of Australia's very lucrative tourism industry.

On top of all that, a report in 2009 revealed that £80 billion of property was at risk from rising sea levels and more frequent storms. This has sent something of a shockwave down the backbones of the 80 per cent of Australian citizens who live along the coastline. And few politicians know what to do with the report's principal policy proposal that there should be a ban on *any* further development at beach level.

So what has been the net impact of all these shocks on Australian politics? The victory of Kevin Rudd over John Howard in the last general election was attributed in part to his relatively progressive stance on climate change. But since then, there's been one setback after another for his government, in terms of introducing appropriate policy interventions, with Australia's mining industries in full-on defensive mode. The equivalent of the CBI in Australia has been acting exactly like the CBI did under the Neanderthal leadership of Digby Jones, a few years ago, with its head stuck firmly in the sand.

This has caused difficulty within the governing party, and has split the opposition party down the middle, causing the resignation in 2009 of its leader, and bringing to an end Kevin Rudd's laborious efforts to fashion a consensus-based agreement on a new (and extremely modest!) cap-and-trade scheme. The parliamentary process is now entirely gridlocked.

Against this backdrop, the only conclusion one can come to realistically is that the shocks to the political system in Australia simply have not been traumatic enough. The pain associated directly with accelerating climate change has not yet reached what might be described as a *political* (rather than a scientific) tipping point – which gives us some idea of just how bad things are going to have to get, all around the world, but particularly in the rich world, and even more particularly in the USA, before electorates finally empower their politicians to start getting serious about transforming our economies.

I want to explore what I believe to be the principal reasons for this kind of mismatch between the politicians and their electorates – the reason why there is still relatively little buy-in from so many citizens – even in those countries where climate change has been widely discussed over many years. I will argue that it's all to do with the wider discourse around climate change – the way it is being framed in terms of public and media debate.

One way of looking at this conundrum is as a set of Russian Matryoshka dolls, but in reverse! Instead of starting with the biggest doll and working down to the smallest doll, I want to look at five 'framing discourses' from the inside out, looking at how each of these is nested within a much broader philosophical discourse. That means starting with the smallest doll of all (often described by politicians as 'climate change as an environmental issue'), working through to the great big mother doll ('climate change as the biggest philosophical transformation since the Enlightenment'), within which all the other climate change dolls are contained.

The starting point ('climate change as an environmental issue') lies in the origins of the climate discourse back in the late 1970s and early 1980s, involving a grouping of eminent earth scientists and environmental NGOs. From that point on, climate change has invariably been described by the media as 'an environmental issue'. That is understandable, but also a completely ridiculous misperception. More and more people now recognise that climate change is about a lot more than the environment: economics, security, culture, behaviour change, geopolitics, the future of human civilisation and so on.

The next layer out is to characterise climate change as a 'resource efficiency issue'. This is the favoured frame for politicians trying to cope with the implications of accelerating climate change without having to look too deeply into the true economic consequences. They know that the vast majority of people still want all the benefits of today's economic growth but without the externalities (as economists describe them) in terms of the emissions of greenhouse gases. So the solution, we are told, is to decouple the desirable objective of economic growth from the undesirable consequence of emissions, through huge improvements in resource efficiency and equally huge reductions in CO_2 intensity – the amount of CO_2 emitted for each unit of GDP.

This is where most governments have got to. Not just the EU, Japan and the USA, but China and India too. David Miliband, Foreign Secretary in the UK, is very upbeat about the potential in this: 'high growth, low emissions' is how he captures the challenge. And that is basically what the Copenhagen process at the end of 2009 was all about: how best to continue to improve people's lives through rising levels of economic growth without the civilisation-threatening build-up of greenhouse gases in the atmosphere.

One part of this particular framing of climate change is certainly true: we do indeed need full-on decoupling. Urgently. In every sector of the economy, in every country. Politicians have been talking about it for a very long time, but there is still relatively little going on to deliver it.

But people have no idea about the scale of what is being proposed here in terms of this decoupling challenge. If we take the widely agreed long-term target of reducing emissions of greenhouse gases by 80 per cent by 2050 – many countries (including the USA) are now signing up to that kind of ambition level. What would that mean, practically, in terms of what has become the most useful 'decoupling indicator', namely the amount of CO_2^e

(looking at the whole basket of greenhouse gases) emitted for every dollar of economic output? In his wonderful new book *Prosperity without Growth?*, Professor Tim Jackson explains what the 80 per cent target means in terms of $CO_2^e/\$$.[1]

Right now, looking at the global economy as a whole, we emit 768g of CO_2^e for every dollar. To achieve an 80 per cent reduction, all other things being equal, we would need to get that down to 36g by 2050. If we wanted everyone in the world to be able to enjoy the same kind of standard of living as we do in the OECD today, we would need to get down to 14g. And if we ourselves are hoping that our already wealthy economies can continue to grow (at roughly 2 per cent per annum over the next 40 years), then the CO_2^e intensity target comes down to an eye-watering 6g. From 768g $CO2^e/\$$ to 6g $CO2^e/\$$.

That is the harsh reality of the ever-so-reassuring notion of decoupling. That is why former Vice-President Al Gore described the truth of climate change as 'inconvenient'!

Indeed, it is so inconvenient that the vast majority of politicians refuse to acknowledge that this is actually the scale of the problem. It is perfectly acceptable, within today's dominant model of progress, to frame climate change in terms of ramping up policy interventions to improve resource efficiency, but few if any have the remotest idea of what this actually means in practice.

Which means we must now move on to the third of our Russian dolls. Climate change is clearly misrepresented both as 'an environmental issue' and as 'a resource efficiency issue'. Looking at it from a macro-economic perspective, we must now ask whether the prevailing consensus (that managing climate change and simultaneously maintaining high levels of economic growth are completely compatible) has any remaining credibility whatsoever.

Back in 2000, Professor Paul Ekins undertook the most comprehensive analysis to date of the degree to which a genuinely sustainable, near-zero carbon economy might be reconciled with the pursuit of conventional economic growth. *Economic Growth and Environmental Sustainability* came to the following conclusion:

It is clear from past experience that the relationship between the economy's value and its physical scale is variable, and that it is possible to reduce the material intensity of GNP. *This establishes the theoretical possibility of GNP growing indefinitely in a finite material world.* However, neither such a possibility nor previous experience says much about the kind of change in the physical impacts of current economic activity which are required for that activity to become environmentally sustainable *in the real world.*[2]

If we are serious about the scale of the decoupling challenge laid out above, we have to accept the real world for what it is, not what we would like it to be.

My conclusion here is a simple one: year-on-year increases in consumption-driven conventional economic growth, for more and more hundreds of people, indefinitely into the future, is simply not compatible with the idea of a sustainable, ultra-low carbon economy. And that means we are going to have to fundamentally rethink the conventional growth model on which the global economy is currently based.

There is no time to dig down any deeper into this critical area of enquiry. But the current debate about alternatives to the dominant growth paradigm is getting richer all the time. Tim Jackson's *Prosperity without Growth?* provides the best possible way of getting into this debate, and the 2009 report (*Report on the Measurement of Economic Performance and Social Progress*), authored by Amartya Sen and Joseph Stiglitz for President Sarkozy, has moved things on even further. As President Sarkozy so succinctly put it on launching the Report, we simply have to 'free ourselves of our current GDP fetishism'.

Once we start getting serious about alternative macro-economic models (without which I do not believe it is possible to get serious about radically decarbonising the economy), then we also have to get serious about the fourth of our Matryoshka dolls – namely, equity. One of the putative benefits of year-on-year economic growth has been the promise that with the economic 'pie' getting bigger and bigger all the time, there would be more every year not just for the already well-off but for the poor –

through increased job opportunities (generated by general increases in wealth and higher levels of consumption), improved public services, and (as the last resort) improved welfare safety nets.

And that has sort of worked – at least in those countries that believe that disparities in wealth should be actively managed to limit social injustice. In such countries, redistribution is not a dirty word. In countries that do not believe this (including, I am sorry to say, both my own and yours), year-on-year increases in economic growth have done much less to improve the lot of the poor, so that social injustice and lack of social mobility remain grave and persistent problems.

With much lower levels of economic growth, those equity issues will become even starker – and the need for redistributive interventions (through fiscal and public expenditure policies) even more persuasive.

There is a particularly compelling aspect of this as it relates to accelerating climate change and the way in which we frame our understanding of that pervasive phenomenon. Increasingly, policy makers are starting to think about climate change in terms of 'the global commons' affected by it. The 'commons' in question refer to the physical capacity of different ecosystems (atmospheric, terrestrial and marine) to absorb the greenhouse gases that we emit.

That capacity is obviously limited. At the moment, different countries command a different share of that capacity on the basis of their historical and *current* per capita emissions. Around 20 tonnes per annum, on average, if you're a citizen of the USA; 0.6 tonnes if you're a citizen of India. Historically speaking, that's just the way it is. But on what basis should access to this all-important global commons be allocated in future? With the same per capita allocations locked in indefinitely (or 'grandfathered', as some describe it)? Or on a strictly equal per capita basis, with each citizen of Planet Earth entitled to exactly the same 'share of resource' as a simple matter of natural justice?

Logically, the latter dispensation (per capita equality) must be the morally correct basis on which to determine future international agreements on climate change. But the difficult second-order issue that flows from that moral position then becomes paramount: over what period of time will it be possible and/or necessary to achieve this convergence? As you can imagine, leaders of rich world countries are more than a little reluctant to get drawn into this debate, although it is clear that any serious proposal for a *global* trading scheme will not be able to ignore this issue.

From that perspective, our fourth Matryoshka doll ('climate change framed as an equity challenge') clearly goes a lot further than climate change as an environmental issue or climate change as a resource efficiency issue, or even climate change as a question of alternative macro-economic models. For people listening to the Chinese and Indian leaders at Copenhagen, one stark reality became clear: there will be no durable solution to accelerating climate change that is not based on the principle of fairness for the world's poor. Which means, paradoxically, that climate change may just become the means by which wealth is redistributed (via 'fair shares in carbon') more effectively than any other.

Daunting though it is, we have to stick with the logic here. If climate change is indeed the single most serious threat to the future of humankind (as *many* scientists and politicians now believe), then the solutions to it will necessarily transform every aspect of our lives. The kind of radical decarbonisation that is required will inevitably mandate not just a wholly different macro-economic paradigm (one that is not based on consumption-driven economic growth indefinitely into the future), but a wholly different approach to global equity. And that will require the emergence of a wholly different *model of progress* – my fifth and final Matryoshka doll!

The basic premise underlying our current model of progress is simple, all but universal (with a few exceptions such as North Korea and Cuba) and very deeply embedded: material improvements both in the lives of individuals and for each nation can be secured *solely* (it is argued) through exponential increases in year-on-year economic growth. Without such growth, progress is judged to be unattainable; with it, progress becomes possible, depending on the integrity and vitality of the governance systems involved in each country.

As I have argued above, the model has 'worked' well enough for the fortunate 1 or 1.5 billion that currently command the lion's share of net global wealth and assets – just so long as you avert your eyes from the devastation of the natural world that it has simultaneously brought about, and from the continuing misery of the world's 2 or 3 billion poorest people. Factor in what we now know about the likely impact of accelerating climate change, and it becomes incontrovertibly clear that our current model of progress cannot possibly work for another 5 billion human beings today, let alone for the extra 2.5 billion who will be joining us here on Earth between now and 2050.

Again, there's clearly no space in an article of this kind to enter into a sophisticated debate about *alternative models of progress*. But the literature on this from within the Green Movement, going back over the last 30 years, is voluminous. Suffice it to say, for the time being, that today's growth-obsessed paradigm of progress has pushed all such alternatives to the margins of political debate. The Green Party, for instance, may find that it now has a much more welcoming context within which to explore its more radical *policies*. But it still finds it infinitely harder to open up any kind of deeper debate about underlying *models of progress*.

And perhaps that is not so surprising. If one skims over some of the key elements in any contrast of different models, it rapidly becomes clear just how profound a philosophical transformation would be required: moving away from debt-driven economic growth to needs-based economic development; from conspicuous consumption to material modesty; from fetishising GDP to a consistent focus on well-being and flourishing; from near-total dependency on fossil fuels to near-total reliance on solar technologies; from continuing denial of any physical limits (regarding either population growth or growth in the economy) to a society that works within and celebrates those limits; from metaphors of domination and mastery over the Earth to an ethic of stewardship and the practice of cohabitation.

That kind of transformation is precisely what today's politicians are so keen to avoid any discussion of. Which is why it is much more convenient for them to frame climate change either as an 'environmental issue' or as a 'resource efficiency challenge', both of which can be managed without needing to ask citizens to rethink their entire lives!

If only it were that simple. Any dispassionate analysis of the scale of the challenge involved tells us something very different: that we are unlikely to make much progress in addressing climate change as an environmental issue without understanding the reality of what 'radical decarbonisation' actually means. We're unlikely to achieve that kind of radical decarbonisation without jettisoning the kind of growth-at-all-costs that has dominated our lives for the last 50 years or so. And we will not do that until we have internalised the uncomfortable truth that life on a carbon-constrained planet is one that will demand a dramatic narrowing of the gaps between the rich and the poor, both within nations and between nations. And how likely is that outcome while our model of progress remains fundamentally misaligned with the non-negotiable physical realities that confront our species at this point in its evolution?

As we have seen, politicians today are trying to strike the right note of urgency on climate change, but remain very perplexed at the continuing confusion on the part of their citizens. As a result, they often end up offering starker and starker warnings of what will happen if we don't start 'acting on CO_2'. As it happens, Act on CO_2 is the name of the communications campaign run by the UK government to get people doing more to reduce their carbon footprint.

As part of this campaign, shock-horror tactics are very much part of the deal. The latest television advert features Dad reading a bedtime story to his daughter. The story is all about climate change, and the terrible things that are about to happen to us as temperatures soar and sea levels rise. As her teddy bear sinks beneath the all-engulfing tidal wave, her eyes widen with fear: 'Does this story have a happy ending, Daddy?' 'That depends on us,' he says.

Like hell it does! *Of course* we can all do our bit, and it's really important that more and more of us do. And that this bit gets bigger and bigger. But only governments can regulate markets and reframe today's macro-economic model to ensure sustainable, ultra-low-carbon outcomes from that economy. You cannot dump responsibility for transforming the entire global economy on the shoulders of a six-year-old child who's just lost her teddy bear.

I believe it's that 'agency problem' (who should bear the responsibility for doing what against the backdrop of accelerating climate change) that lies at the heart of people's continuing scepticism. At a workshop convened in October 2009 by the UK government to consult on climate change, one participant gave vent to her frustration with this cry of angst: 'Climate change just can't be as bad as you're telling me it is – otherwise there would be mass hysteria across the entire country!'

There well might. But people intuitively suspect either that things cannot be as bad as they are told they are (in which case, there's no need for emergency action on their part, and just turning off the lights is fine), or that they really *are* that bad, in which case the government should be doing a great deal more than simply asking them to turn off their lights. If things are that bad, why isn't the government demonstrating complete consistency in the portfolio of policies it brings forward – instead of pushing ahead with plans for another runway at Heathrow and new coal-fired power stations, and widening congested motorways? As we say here in the UK, 'they smell a rat'. Psychologists refer to it as 'systemic cognitive dissonance'.

It is hard not to feel more than the occasional spasm of sympathy for world leaders as they struggle with the very idea of 'the environment at the crossroads'. They haven't even got anyone to blame for the way in which decades of environmental dereliction have caught up with us, after years of both denial and deliberate misrepresentation. There is no enemy out there; rather, it's our way of life (to which most of us are very firmly wedded) that lies at the heart of the problem.

So what are our chances of securing a sustainable future for our species? 'In the balance', is really all one can say. Thirty-five years on from the early diagnosis of our environmental troubles at the 1972 United Nations Conference on the Environment and Human Development in Stockholm, we've really made very little

progress. And as I said before, were it not for the unignorable challenge that accelerating climate change now confronts us with, I
rather suspect that we would try to carry on for another 35 years
in exactly the same way as we have for the last.

But as a result of our burgeoning awareness of the potential
consequences of climate change, we know that we have now got
just a few years left to set in train two parallel transitions on which
the future of our species depends: the transition from fossil fuels
to solar energy, and the transition from societies driven by growth-
at-all-costs to societies where well-being, social justice and
flourishing for all people take precedence.

Which takes us back to our Matryoshka dolls. Sooner or later,
we have got to accept climate change for what it really is: *not* 'an
environmental issue', but the last, best chance to transform our
inherently cruel and unsustainable model of progress before it's
too late.

Notes

1 Tim Jackson, *Prosperity without Growth: Economics for a Finite Planet*
   (London: Earthscan, 2009).
2 Paul Ekins, *Economic Growth and Environmental Sustainability: The
   Prospects for Green Growth* (London: Routledge, 1999).

Conference Programme

Environment at the Crossroads

International Conference
Calouste Gulbenkian Foundation, 27–28 October 2009

Tuesday, 27 October

9h30 | *Opening Session*
Emílio Rui Vilar
President of the Calouste Gulbenkian Foundation

Viriato Soromenho-Marques
Scientific Coordinator of the Gulbenkian Environment
Programme

José Manuel Durão Barroso [Video]
President of the European Commission

Opening Lecture
David King
Director, Smith School for Enterprise and the Environment,
Oxford
Climate Change as a Global Shifting Force

14h30 | *The State of the Environment and its Societal Dimensions*
Moderator: **George Polk**
Managing Partner, Soros Climate Fund Management, London

Miguel Araújo
Museo Nacional de Ciencias Naturales de Madrid
University of Évora
Has Biodiversity a Future?

Pedro Arrojo Agudo
University of Zaragoza
The Ethical Imperative of Sustainability in Water Management

José Lima Santos
Technical University of Lisbon
The Environmental Crisis and the Future of Agriculture

17h00 | *Keynote Address*
Chairman: **António Pinto Ribeiro**
Gulbenkian Programme, Next Future

Gilles Lipovetsky
Philosopher and Professor, University of Grenoble
Hyper-consumer Society and Happiness

Wednesday, 28 October

9h30 | *The State of the Environment and its Economic Dimensions*

Moderator: **Susana Fonseca**
President, Quercus – National Association for Nature
Conservation, Lisbon

Allan Larsson
Chairman, Lund University
Europe, the USA and China after the Crisis: Towards New Growth Models for Sustainability?

Malini Mehra
CEO, Centre for Social Markets, Delhi
Citizen Action on Climate Change and Sustainable Development

Pedro Martins Barata
Executive Board Member, Clean Development Mechanism
Consultant, Portuguese Climate Change Commission
Emissions Trading Schemes and the Future of the Carbon Economy

11h30 | *Keynote Address*
Chairman: **João Falcato**
CEO, Oceanário de Lisboa

Julie Packard
Executive Director, Monterey Bay Aquarium, California
Charting a Course for the Future of the Oceans: Present State and Future Perspectives

14h30 | *Governance Towards Sustainability*
Moderator: **David Silva e Sousa**
Director, Centre of Studies and Strategies for Sustainability, Lisbon

Nitin Desai
Formerly Under-Secretary General in the United Nations
Distinguished Fellow, The Energy and Resources Institute, India
Governance for Sustainable Development: A Perspective

Alex Ellis
British Ambassador in Lisbon
Climate Change: The Perspective from Europe

Miranda Schreurs
Environmental Policy Research Centre, Freie Universität Berlin
A New Sustainability Politics under the Obama Administration:
Progress and Obstacles

17h00 | *Keynote Address*
Chairman: **Luísa Schmidt**
Sociologist, Senior Researcher at the Institute of Social Sciences
University of Lisbon

Jonathon Porritt
President, Forum for the Future, London
What are the Prospects for a Sustainable Future?

18h00 | *Closing Session*

Emílio Rui Vilar
President of the Calouste Gulbenkian Foundation

Viriato Soromenho-Marques
Scientific Coordinator of the Gulbenkian Environment
Programme

Acknowledgements

Environment at the Crossroads: Aiming for a Sustainable Future presents the proceedings of the Conference of the same name, which took place at the Calouste Gulbenkian Foundation, in Lisbon, during 27–28 October 2009.

The Conference, with the subsequent book, was an initiative of the President of the Calouste Gulbenkian Foundation, Emílio Rui Vilar, developed under the scientific coordination of Viriato Soromenho-Marques and with the technical and executive support of Rui Esgaio, Elisabete Caramelo, Rui Gonçalves and Ana Barcelos Pereira.